W9-AXA-792

ADIOS ARGENTINA
XMAS
1934

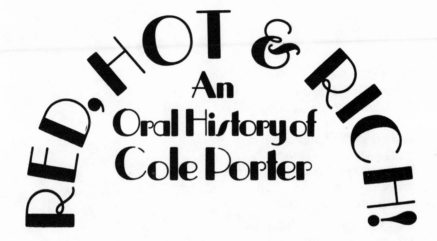

RED, HOT & RICH!
An Oral History of Cole Porter

David Grafton

STEIN AND DAY/*Publishers*/New York

Endpaper

A caricature of Cole Porter at the piano by French artist SEM engraved on a 14-K gold Cartier cigarette case. It reads: ADIOS ARGENTINA, X'MAS 1934, and was commissioned by the composer. *(AP/Wide World Photos)*

First published in 1987
Copyright © 1987 by David Grafton
All rights reserved, Stein and Day, Incorporated
Designed by Louis A. Ditizio
Printed in the United States of America
STEIN AND DAY/*Publishers*
Scarborough House
Briarcliff Manor, N.Y. 10510
IN THE UNITED STATES
Distributed to the Trade By
Henry Holt and Company, Inc.
521 Fifth Avenue
New York, N.Y. 10175

IN CANADA
Distributed by
Fitzhenry & Whiteside Limited
195 Allstate Parkway
Markham, Ontario
Canada L3R 4TA
Library of Congress Cataloging-in-Publication Data

Grafton, David.
  Red, hot and rich!

  1. Porter, Cole, 1891–1964.   2. Composers—
United States—Biography.   I. Title.
ML410.P7844G7 1987   782.81'092'4   [B]   86-42684
ISBN 0-8128-3112-8

For
George Chapman, Moreatha Ellis,
Hon. Rafael Hernandez Colon, Jewel LaFontant, Luis Ortiz,
Florence Stern, Salvador (Chiry) Vassallo,
Margarita G. Vincenty, and Doris L. Zollar

Contents

List of Illustrations

Prelude

HOW DOES A Hoosier hick from Peru, Indiana, become the quintessential American composer of his generation and the darling of international society?

Despite being born in America's heartland, Cole Porter became the ultimate sophisticate of his day. He was a rich nobody from the hayseed hinterlands who made his way east and succeeded in taking the gilded citadel by storm.

The success of Cole Porter's musicals, with songs from the erotic "Love for Sale" to the bouncy "Anything Goes," plus his limitless personal charisma and his utter enthusiasm for going places, doing things, and generally being fascinating to everyone he met were the component parts in a rich-to-riches life that had no counterpart in the contemporary theater.

Prior to a tragic accident and on a limited basis afterward, there was seldom a private party of account that Porter missed during the months he spent in New York, and if he could be induced by his hostess to sit down at the piano and play a few of his clever and catchy songs, the evening became part of history.

The hold that Cole Porter exerted on the imagination and

loyalties of a vast and sophisticated following was chiefly attributed to that elusive quality—charm. To him the word was an immense joke and was never to be treated seriously.

Although an accident left him a virtual cripple for the rest of his life, he remained amazingly youthful and productive for more than two decades. Cole Porter had no peer as a composer and lyricist and international celebrity—he was the Number One darling of Café Society.

Playboy, expatriate, first-nighter, highbrow, and homosexual. These are words that only skim the surface in describing the highly complex and talented Cole Porter.

COLE PORTER'S EVOLUTION took a circuitous route that included a wealthy grandfather, a determined, society-conscious mother, a proper Eastern preparatory school, Yale University, a try at Harvard Law School, and finally travels to all the glamour spots of the world (and some not so glamorous), and a trip to the altar to marry an older, dazzling divorcée. When he married, he became a member of the international social set that had its headquarters in Paris: their house at 13 rue Monsieur was the ultimate stopping-off place for resident expatriates and visiting Americans, and had a guest list that often contained the names of Winston Churchill, Artur Rubenstein, and the Prince of Wales.

It was from these beginnings that Cole Porter went on to become the musical voice of the 1930s' Café Society crowd. He would continue writing unforgettable songs for the theater and films for the next three decades.

Brooke Astor, his friend for thirty-six years, calls him a very complex man. It was this complex nature that gave us a stunning array of music. Cole Porter single-handedly provided the words and music for thirty-three stage musicals, numerous films, and a television production. No other American composer has ever matched his record. That record includes "Begin the Beguine," "Night and Day," "You Do Something to Me," "I Get a Kick Out of You," and such memorable shows as *Kiss Me, Kate, Anything Goes,* and *Can-Can.*

Having grown up at the feet of a dazzling flapper-era mother, I became a devotee of Cole Porter's music early on. As a result, Cole Porter's name and his music were all part of a certain mystique associated with a time, and a frame of mine associated with a devil-may-care attitude in a world with simpler values.

Years later, my first meeting with the legend was wonderfully serendipitous. I was a guest at a dinner party held in the now-extinct Colony restaurant in New York. As we finished dinner, Rosie Dolly, my dinner hostess, received a note from Cole Porter inviting Miss Dolly and her guests to join him and his guests at his table for coffee and after-dinner drinks. The evening was to make a very lasting impression upon my young self; I would later be fortunate to visit him in his New England country home.

WHEN, DECADES AFTER, I had an irresistible desire to write a book about the fascinating playboys and playgirls of the 1930s, I was advised by a friend in publishing to select one subject from that period. Since I had met Cole Porter on a number of occasions and the music and the man's life-style stayed with me all those years, my multi-subject topic evolved into a select and unique one. Several years of researching and writing have produced this book.

David Grafton
Chicago, Illinois

1

"It's Awful Hard When Mother's Not Along"

A VERY HOT June 9, 1891, saw the arrival of Cole Porter in his parents' rambling, frame Victorian house at the corner of East Third and Huntington streets in Peru, Indiana. The son of Kate Cole and Samuel Fenwick Porter was to be raised in an atmosphere of both love and fear. The love came from his snobbish, overly indulgent mother; the fear from his grandfather, James Omar (J.O.) Cole. J.O. was a tyrannical millionaire scornful of the niceties of life, except when it came to his own comfort and the comfort of his immediate family.

Early in the marriage, Cole's parents had suffered the loss of their first two children; a young son, Louis, died in 1885, and a two-year-old daughter, Rachel, died in 1890. When Cole arrived on that June day, he entered a family troubled by uncertainty, loss, and tension. The loss of the two earlier children and Cole's physical resemblance to Kate perhaps in part accounted for her strong love and determination to see that this son's life must make its mark.

From the beginning, Kate took charge of raising her son in her own sensitive but extravagant image, ignoring every suggestion from her husband and rarely heeding any from her all-powerful father. She dressed Cole fussily in starched shirt-blouses trimmed with lace cuffs. In winter he was dressed in fur and velvet wraps when taken outdoors.

If Kate could not find the latest in finery for Cole at the John S. Hale & Co. department store in Peru, she ordered his clothes from Marshall Field & Co. in Chicago. Photographs still exist of Cole in the most elaborate and expensive clothing, which give the young lad a definite feminine air.

Kate also discouraged Cole from ball-playing and any form of roughhousing. While other Indiana boys were busy robbing birds' nests, he wrote songs about the feathered friends, accompanying himself on the violin and piano. He composed his first song at the age of ten, calling it "The Song of the Birds," and his second, "The Bobolink Waltz," at age twelve. He dedicated both compositions to his mother.

Cole Porter's Peru revolved around his family and the advantages they gave him as a boy, as scion of a wealthy but socially negligible clan from a remote Indiana town. Local legend developed about Cole, who cut a dandy figure as he arrived mornings at his elementary school atop his pedigreed pony and dressed in a Buster Brown suit, black patent leather shoes, and straw boater.

J. O. Cole, his grandfather, was a self-made millionaire whose business included vast lumber, coal, and gas holdings in West Virginia, Illinois, and Indiana; it was both work and play. J.O. drove himself hard and expected no less from others in his pursuit of wealth. He is remembered for his terrible temper and his loathing for wasteful living. Home was a different story for J.O. There he treated the women of his family with great love and generosity, and the relationship between father and daughter was especially close. It was also complicated since J.O. had little interest or respect for the cultural aspects of life that so attracted Kate. And when J.O. Cole placed Kate on the marriage market it was no surprise that he was disappointed when she chose a penniless, dreamy young druggist with a fondness for the poetry of Robert Browning and the theories of horticulturist Luther Burbank.

In the early years of her marriage Kate was deliriously happy with Samuel Fenwick Porter, especially since Sam proved to be so malleable. Kate made every effort to bring her father and husband closer together, which resulted in at least an outward show of friendliness on their part. Years later, J.O. built a big house for the Porters on Westleigh Farms* and provided Sam with an Isotta limousine. For everyday use, however, Sam continued to drive a small runabout for the simple reason that much of the time he did not have enough money to supply gas for the luxury car.

Kate chose to ignore the family's lack of pedigree; she was determined that her only surviving child would be identified with the upper stratum of society (or what passed for society in a backwater town like Peru, Indiana). Cole attributed her attendance at church every Sunday to her desire to be seen in her finery.

"I never felt religion was serious to her," Cole recalled years later. "It was of no importance. She just went to show off her new hats."

Kate's program of "upper-class" refinements for Cole included studying violin, piano, and French. She engaged her dressmaker, Mme. Cattin, originally from Dijon, France, to tutor him in French.

Mme. Cattin believed Cole was an apt pupil because he possessed perfect musical pitch; this made it simple for him to mimic her accent. The brilliance of Kate's only child reinforced his mother's determination that Cole should pursue a career as a musician. Cole, only six at the time, disliked the violin but

*Contrary to what Cole told his friends at Worcester and Yale about living in a big house surrounded by an apple orchard, the Porters did not move into the newly built mansion at Westleigh Farms until 1910.

took immediately to the piano, although he hated the two hours of daily practice forced upon him by his mother.

Meanwhile, Kate distracted herself by taking up with a gypsy numerologist, who convinced her that any person whose initials spelled out a simple word would achieve success in life. Kate hurried down to the Miami County Courthouse and extended her son's name officially from Cole Porter to Cole Albert Porter—C.A.P., cap. At the same time, she changed the year of his birth from 1891 to 1893; when Cole went away to school years later, he would appear to be a precocious twelve year old rather than a merely mature fourteen year old.

The year 1897 marked a turning point for six-year-old Cole. It was the year he made his first journey to the outside world, beyond the boundaries of Peru and Miami County, and it would set a pattern for a lifetime of nomadic habits.

The purpose of these train trips was to further Cole's musical education at the Marion, Indiana, Conservatory of Music thirty miles away. At first, Cole enjoyed the novelty of these trips and the freedom they offered away from the constant gaze of his mother, but within a short time Cole became bored. However, he soon found a diversion to break the monotony of commuting and the six-hour wait between trains.

Candy sellers in Marion offered more than the usual sweets; they also carried a large selection of spicy books, the sort that were automatically forbidden to young people in Indiana. After his lessons, Cole would stock up on this risque material. The lyrics in a number of Cole Porter's songs owe a debt to these naughty books, especially "But in the Morning, No!," "Nobody's Changing Me," "My Heart Belongs to Daddy," "Always True to You (In My Fashion)," and "Love For Sale," a song considered absolutely indecent when it came out in 1930.

Neither Cole's grandfather nor his powerless father had much input regarding the boy's musical education. J.O. of course considered such "sissy" pursuits a waste of time, while

Sam seemed not to care at all, with one exception—Cole's father read to him and passed on to him the poetry of Robert Browning, Lord Byron, and Percy Bysshe Shelley. And Cole put this early exposure to the poets to good use when composing his sophisticated lyrics in his adult life.

J.O.'s reaction to his grandson's musical interests can be summed up in a statement he made to a business associate during this period: "I don't like all this music business. If the boy becomes a lawyer, I'll leave him my money. If he does not, he gets nothing."

This opposition from her father did not stop Kate in her mission to create a musical genius. Once a year, she imported the Marion Conservatory Orchestra to Peru, bought out the entire house, and distributed tickets to friends and store owners in the area.

Prior arrangements that Kate had made with the orchestra's conductor saw to it that Cole would be invited to perform a violin solo. Friends and townfolk alike took little pride in the budding genius; contrary to what Kate had hoped, Cole became the butt of jokes among his young friends, and Kate was severely criticized by her father and her friends.

The only compensation for Cole at this time was that whenever he performed he sensed the great pride Kate took in all this. Each time he acquiesced to her wishes, she rewarded him with a special gift or increased his weekly allowance. It was a ploy that Cole would put to good use in his adult life in order to get what he wanted in professional acclaim and also in his personal relationships.

In 1897, his hometown was still a center of provincialism; it had changed little in the six years since Cole's birth. The church was very important to Peru's early settlers, and most of the citizens were churchgoing people. The churches were highly fundamentalist in outlook and passed that narrow philosophy on to their parishioners.

While most parents followed the precept laid down by their stern ancestors that sparing the rod would spoil the child, this was never Kate's method. She believed in cajoling her young son into following the path she had laid out for him, a path she ardently believed would lead to his becoming a world celebrity.

The picture we get of Cole as a youth can best be remembered from photographs taken of him in the mid-1890s and early 1900s. Cole's small, round face, with its smooth skin, was delicate and boyish and dominated by large, expressive eyes. The wide mouth rarely broke into a smile; rather, it seemed to already show a hint of the smugness he was to exhibit throughout his entire life.

This smugness may well have been his way of being noncommittal, his personal armor against all the pain and dissension surrounding him at home: his mother, a forerunner of the theatrical mother bent on creating a star; the ineffectual father helpless against the family patriarch and escaping into a fantasy world of poets, helped along occasionally by generous doses of his own moonshine whiskey.

The cantankerous J. O. Cole constantly fumed about the son-in-law he neither respected nor understood, and he badgered Kate about the "sissy" way she was raising his grandson. But Kate Porter was more than a match for the husband she had long ago dismissed and for the father upon whom she and her child were almost totally dependent. (Sam Porter's drugstore brought in only a minimum of income; thus daughter and grandson looked to J.O. to supply most of the luxuries that were a part of their life.) As the daughter of the richest man in Peru and one of the richest in Indiana, Kate had to keep up appearances, and all this was supported by her father.

Occasionally, J.O. would play a grandfatherly role and take young Cole aboard his rig, with its fine Kentucky-bred horse leading the way through rural Miami County. On these occasions, J.O. never failed to point out the land and buildings he owned and to impress upon the child just what he would inherit one day provided he followed the path his grandfather was laying out for him.

The companionship of children his own age escaped Cole for the most part. Because of his music lessons and daily practice, his day was so structured that there was little time to be given to recreation and even less time to the aimless pursuits so dear to every boy's heart. However, the summers of Cole's childhood provided some respite from lessons and were filled with family activities: ice-cream socials at home or at the home of his favorite cousin, Desdemona Bearss, whose mother was a great admirer of Shakespeare. Livery dealer George E. Reed often hitched up one of his rubber-tire rigs and stylish horses to take Cole and his own three sons to the banks of the Mississinewa River for a summer picnic.

The Cole and Porter families spent part of each summer at Lake Maxinkuckee, located forty miles north of Peru. It was here in the open country, without the daily piano practice and required reading, that Cole approximated the picture of the typical midwestern youth of his day. There was daily swimming in the crystal-clear lake, and there were excursions and diving parties aboard *The Peerless*, the big lake steamer.

In winter, Cole was allowed to skate on the frozen Wabash River, and on rare occasions Kate allowed him to invite a few select classmates home; here Cole would regale his friends with his toy theater, with its operable stage and changeable sets. He would create a fantasy world, acting out all the parts himself. Although he was far too young to fully appreciate the applause that was rendered him as he mimicked and sang his way through each scene, none of this was lost on his proud mother.

But nothing in Cole's childhood left a greater impression on him than the Great Wallace Show, a circus that wintered in

Peru. The saga of the circus in Peru began a half-dozen years before Cole's birth when a circus owner could not pay his feed bill. Ben Wallace, a livery stable owner with a snake-oil salesman's personality, took over a circus wagon laden with a blind lion, a trained baboon, a cage full of exotic birds, a cage of monkeys, plus all the equipment. During Cole Porter's youth, the circus menagerie had greatly expanded and the eight-year-old Cole gloried in all the razzle-dazzle of circus life. To his young mind it represented a world beyond Peru, away from the often stifling environment found at home. It was a moment of escape for Cole, and Ben Wallace, whom he called "Uncle Ben," allowed Cole free rein at the circus farm. The 38-acre farm became a fairyland of wonder for the impressionable Cole. He loved the circus people, and he would wander through the animal barns asking questions of the keeper, especially about the mating habits he was to chronicle so assiduously ("birds do it, bees do it," etc.) in many of his songs for the stage and screen.

But Cole's favorites were the "freaks" who inhabited the sideshow of every circus: "the Bearded Lady," "the Fat Lady," "the Monkey Boy," and other assorted exhibitionists so familiar to generations of circusgoers. He may even have acquired his occasionally bizarre way of dressing from the denizens of the Great Wallace Show.

Another outlet dear to Cole's heart was the theater. Al Martin brought *Uncle Tom's Cabin* to Peru for thirty-five years, and Cole could always be seen down front at the Wallace Theatre on opening day. Cole also frequented the Emeric Theatre on West Fifth Street, where the minstrel shows and touring troupes of second-rate actors stopped for one-night stands.

If the Emeric was not known for the professional caliber of its itinerant acting troupes, its polychrome curtain rivaled any theater curtain west of the Hudson River. This tattered marvel depicted the Grand Canal of eighteenth-century Venice in all its glory, and Cole took special joy in seeing this great curtain being raised and lowered, letting his already highly developed imagination transport him among the canals and palazzi of Venice. It may have been in the confines of the darkened Emeric Theatre that Cole first dreamed of occupying one of those vast Venetian palazzi.

The linchpin of Kate's grand design for her son's road to glory was a combination of travel and exposure to culture. She firmly believed that ample doses of both rounded out a person socially far more than book learning. With this in mind, she decided to give Cole his first real experience in travel and culture. In 1897, a trip to Chicago—hog butcher of the world and home of the skyscraper—was planned.

Kate planned this first trip and all successive trips to Chicago for maximum effect to impress upon her son that she alone among family members was concerned about his cultural development and to garner his total gratitude.

It was a momentous journey—a week filled with theater, opera, museums, and daily excursions to the Marshall Field & Co. store on State Street.

Despite her son's tender years, Kate never put restrictions on what she considered cultural pursuits, and the pair also took in the review at the Masonic Temple Roof Theatre, which starred the French chanteuse Josephine Sabel, Mary Norman (known as the "Queen of Mimicry"), and Edna Aug, the American Anna Held.

WHILE KATE WAS teaching her son about culture and fashion, J. O. Cole continued to press his plans for Cole's future. The grandfather thought that Cole needed some toughening up to prepare him for life's hard knocks and proposed that Cole should go to military school near home, or to a business school, or even that he take a complete break from school for a while and learn about farming and the responsibilities of managing the family's various interests. Just as Kate had refused to budge in the face of her father's opposition to her marriage, so too did she remain adamant about her wish to send Cole to a boarding school in the East.

When it came time for the twelve-year-old Cole to leave grammar school, a family quarrel erupted. As a result, Kate and her father did not speak to one another for the next two years, and when Cole left Peru, Indiana, for the Worcester Academy in Massachusetts in 1903, he did not return home for three years, nor did his family write to him. For all practical purposes he temporarily became a boy without a family.

Except for the diversion when the circus was in town, Cole had disliked his small-town childhood; now, at his boarding school, he showed little sign that he missed his mother or anyone else from his hometown. In fact, he spoke so rarely about his family that some students at Worcester thought he was an orphan. At his young age this silence seems to indicate that Cole was already aware of the difference between Indiana and the East. It also gave some indication of his social aspirations.

Even though there was no letter-writing between Cole and his family, he did receive a generous allowance, which made him one of the school's wealthier students. He also kept his own upright piano in his private quarters and would perform for his classmates at every opportunity. And although he had been somewhat of a loner and had few friends in Peru, he soon became a favorite of students and faculty at the academy. Cole used the entire spectrum of his personality, musical talent, and energy to ingratiate himself with everyone.

It has been speculated that it was at Worcester that Cole first experimented with homosexuality, but none of my research has turned up any evidence to support these rumors.

If Sam Porter had first aroused Cole's interest in poetry, it would be Worcester Academy's Daniel Webster Abercrombie whom Cole later credited with developing his ability to unify music and text in his songs. Dr. Abercrombie, a dour Scotsman, Harvard-trained, ruled the school in the fashion of a benevolent tyrant. He laid down a prescribed classical curriculum in preparation for college: four years of English and mathematics; three of Greek and Latin; two of French, history, and science, and two years of manual training.

Dr. Abercrombie confined his own teaching to Greek, and as his students attest, he was a marvel at bringing Homer and the other ancient poets to life. Speaking of what he learned from his headmaster as it related to his later work, Cole said, "Words and music must be so inseparably wedded to each other that they are like one." The entire body of Cole Porter's work would be testament to this philosophy.

Under Dr. Abercrombie's watchful eye, Cole applied himself to his studies and did well enough to rate as an honor student, with at least one A and no grade lower than a B for most of his semesters at Worcester. He avoided athletics but participated in numerous other extracurricular activities; he belonged to Sigma Zeta Kappa, the school's highly esteemed debating society, as well as the drama, mandolin, and glee clubs.

If Daniel Webster Abercrombie was a surrogate father, Mrs. Abercrombie was both a surrogate mother and his first real patron. She lent a hand at cultivating good manners in Cole, often inviting him to take tea with her and her husband. She would place a pillow on the piano bench and sit for hours as the boy played selections from contemporary composers.

To ingratiate himself with fellow students, Cole would play renditions of risqué songs of his own like "The Bearded Lady," "The Tattooed Gentleman," and "Fi-Fi Fifi." Unfortunately, no copies of these smutty songs exist today, but from all reports, they were great favorites of Cole's prep school friends.

During his junior year, Cole was elected president of the Mandolin Club and was cast in the leading role of his class play. It was under his persuasion that the class chose Richard Sheridan's *The Rivals*, and Cole was seriously considering becoming an actor. The notices in his school paper gave Cole a good review: "Cole Porter, as Bob Acres, was excellent. He was the carefree young man at first, then the bold fighter, known to the country as 'Fighting Bob,' and last the terrified duelist wishing to receive the fire on his side and shaking with fear. He was full of life and vim throughout."

Notwithstanding that excellent notice, Cole realized that the acting game depended on too many variables. It was then that he decided that writing songs would be his profession. But Cole never lost the actor's ego and the sense of showmanship that went with it.

IN JUNE OF 1908, Cole took the preliminary entrance examination for Yale. He did poorly, and it was suggested that he spend the summer being tutored in New Haven. His grandfather, however, was adamant that he return to Peru.

His mother and grandfather had settled their quarrel, and Cole returned to Indiana, his first trip home since going east. But rather than staying in Peru for an eventual confrontation with J.O., he opted to spend as much time as possible at Lake Maxinkuckee with his Bearss cousins and the family of his boyhood friend, Tommy Hendricks.

TOMMY HENDRICKS: I was Cole Porter's original one-man public, outside of his father and his mother. Of course, his grandfather, J. O. Cole, couldn't see much to this piano playing. He knew that Cole was smart and quick, so he figured that he ought to make a successful farmer, or perhaps even a lawyer. This piano stuff he felt sure was merely a kid fancy that Cole would outgrow.

For years Cole and I went wherever our bicycles and his pony could take us. Suddenly we found that the automobile gave us a whole new range of action. Instead of going out along the river to picnic, we found that in an automobile we could go to Wabash or Logansport or Kokomo and get back to Peru before dark.

Country clubs were rather new affairs in midland Indiana, but we soon learned that they had good meals and a playable piano so we patronized them, although they generally made us wear cut coats [cutaways] in the dining room.

Our entourage was always made up of Des Bearss and Cole and me. Besides her, we would have some other girl, usually Georgianna Wilson, of whom I was very fond even though she was my cousin, Katherine Kenny, Ada Bruff, or Kate Cox, for I was considered the rotating kind.

The Logansport Country Club became our favorite hangout. It is not one of those stark, formal, colonial structures perched on a treeless rise and surrounded by an eighteen-hole golf course that keeps the club constantly in the red. Friendly, simple, and rustic, the Logansport clubhouse rests, cool and comfortable, under towering sycamores on an island between the forks of the Wabash River.

HIS COUSIN, DESDEMONA Bearss, had become a mature, witty girl and shared Cole's interest in music and theater. Des admired his sophistication, polished manners, and talent; she may even have had an innocent crush on this cousin. Before returning to Worcester, Cole invited Des to be his senior prom date.

BY THE END of the spring semester of 1909, Cole learned that he was to be class valedictorian, and he wired his mother immediately. Kate saw to it that Cole's academic achievements were reported in the Peru newspapers. One of these announcements went on to say that "Cole is probably the youngest boy in his class, which numbers at least fifty students, and his selection is quite a distinction."

Again, the question of Cole's age surfaces and leaves little doubt that Kate did indeed change his birthdate from 1891 to 1893. Throughout his adult life Cole would often give his age based upon the later date, lending some credence to rumors that he was aware of and went along with his mother's deception.

J. O. Cole's original reservations about Cole's schooling were tempered somewhat by the boy's good standing, and in a brief message sent to Cole dated May 20, 1909, he unbent enough to write, "The news of your selection we all rejoice in. This fixes the Paris trip."

This trip was one that Cole had clearly campaigned for, using Kate as his emissary. He further placated his grandfather by taking a second set of entrance examinations for Yale just before setting sail for France. This time the results were more successful.

In Paris, Cole stayed with the Delarues family at 29 rue Boissonade, and became adept in conversing in French. Later, he joined several Worcester classmates for a tour of the French countryside and went on to visit Switzerland and Germany. At summer's end, Cole returned to the United States a confirmed Francophile and with a taste for travel.

Worcester had represented the first opportunity for Cole to escape the home nest; now this first trip abroad reinforced his desire for total independence.

2

From Hick to Highbrow

WHEN COLE PORTER entered Yale in the fall of 1909, he was determined to be different. From the very moment that he set foot on the Yale campus, he would follow the pattern that proved so successful earlier—using his musical talent to enhance his social standing. That he came to be known as the personification of Eastern, cosmopolitan sophistication is all the more remarkable, considering his solidly small-town, grass-roots middle-America background.

He was no longer the tousle-haired preppie from the Worcester Academy. His hair was slicked down and parted in the middle in the manner of a French gigolo ready for work (a style he must have picked up on his prep school tour of France). His attire also created quite a bit of comment around campus: plaid suits, pink and yellow shirts, and the most garish ties. No college or regimental stripes for him—not at this point in his life, anyway.

It is not surprising that Cole had to take inventory, assess some of his shortcomings and make some adjustments, as he moved into Garland's Rooming House at 242 York Street. Classmate W. Averell Harriman and others rooming at Garland's found Cole somewhat unsophisticated but appreciated him for his musical talent.

Cole, of course, did not simply sing and play his way through Yale while he was there. But as a result of the emphasis he placed on his social life, his academic record during his freshman year was dismal. He could hardly meet the intellectual expectations of Yale, and even in his music courses he earned mostly C's and D's.

Socially, however, Cole was a star in New Haven. At one time or another he apparently joined nearly every club at Yale: Scroll and Key, the Whiffenpoofs, the Hogans, the Grill Room Grizzlies, the Debating Club, the Mince Pie Club (he was Spice), the Pundits, the Corinthian Yacht Club, the University Club and the Dramatic Association. Quite a record for a Hoosier hick who was determined to transform himself into the ultimate sophisticate of the day.

BROOKE ASTOR: It must have been very hard on Cole when he first went to Yale. Here was Buddie [Brooke Astor's second husband, Charles "Buddie" Marshall] and Averell [Governor W. Averell Harriman] who had roomed together at Groton along with Van [Vanderbilt Webb]; all those Eastern Establishment ties! Yale was not integrated like it is today. Cole was rather the brown leather shoes . . . type. They all thought, "My goodness!" But once he sat down to play the piano, he charmed them right off the bat.

HOWARD CULLMAN: They used to ask whether he was wearing the uniform of Main Street in Peru. But Cole rode it out very well.

AVERELL HARRIMAN: I remember the Yale days with Cole. The first year in New Haven we both lived in Garland's, after that we were in college dormitories. I remember Cole was a bit naive when he first arrived, but we got to admire him greatly because we were thrilled by his music.

Yale was more formal in those days. We had to work hard to pass our exams or else we'd be set back. It was quite strict. Athletics was important: football, of course, was predominant, but I got involved in rowing and eventually coached the Yale crew.

Cole was not involved in athletics, and we drifted apart in the latter part of our college years. I always admired him and kept a relationship throughout, and later knew him in New York.

TOMMY HENDRICKS: Cole Porter definitely was not a football king. He was never to have his picture taken "sitting on the old Yale fence," handsomely bedecked in varsity sweater, although that's just what he desired more than anything else in life.

Yet in an age of Ted Coys and "Lefty" Flynns, when football heroes alone gained the highest rating at Yale, Cole Porter was known to every Yale undergraduate, and by his junior year he had a large, enthusiastic following among the grads.

His fame had risen almost overnight to the lilt of "Bingo Eli Yale," and by his third year he was the recognized leader of most of the musical and theatrical organizations on the campus. One of his big evenings of the entire collegiate year at Yale was the annual production of the Yale Dramatic Association. Cole wrote the songs, staged the performances, and played the leading part. It was the event of the midwinter social calendar and with the whole East Coast all atwitter from Bradford to Sweet Briar, with girls who would have given their joyous sub-deb souls for an invitation from Cole, he asked Des for the event.

Only the night before the show, a finale for one act was needed; Cole sat at the piano in his room and played, for the first time I ever heard it, a song that is the most popular drinking song among all the hundreds sung by college revelers throughout the land. Its lusty words and harmony are sure to be heard during the evening whenever the gang gathers at the Nass at Princeton, the Stardust at Indiana, during the fraternity keg parties at Chapel Hill, North Carolina, the Pretzel Bell at Michigan, or the Tav at the University of Texas.

"For I'm a member of the souse family," Cole carefully tapped out on the keyboard, singing, or rather, in his style, talking the words to the quartet draped around the piano who were to do the song in the show. Then with great gusto he tore into the chorus:

> One keg of beer for the four of us!
> Glory be to God that there are
> no more of us,
> For any of us can drink it all alone.

Immediately the similarity between that and his Bingo struck us all.

> Bingo! Bingo!
> Bingo-bingo-bingo, that's the lingo
> Eli is bound to win.
> There's to be a big victory,
> So watch the team begin.
> Bingo! Bingo!
> Our team shall never fail.
> Fight! Fight! Fight
> with all your might!
> Fight for Bingo, Eli Yale!

Time and tune run almost the same in the two songs. Whether Cole composed the drinking song from his Bingo or

Bingo came from it, perhaps an old English drinking song . . . the star of this particular performance was Cole, one hundred twenty pounds of fire and fight, strutting and striding across the stage in a large, turtleneck sweater adorned with an over-sized "Y," shouting and singing:

> If I were only a football king,
> I'd go punting around all day!

The audience shouted for more—verse upon verse, encore after encore. If varsity letters had been awarded for musical participation and showmanship, Cole would have won his that night. And I guess he was fully confident that he and Yale held the spotlight without any fear of competition from any source, for he arranged to have me squire Des to the show. It was a completely perfect occasion for both Cole and me, for how in the world was either of us to know that evening, as she applauded Cole and smiled so sweetly at me, that Des would do what she did: of all the unbelievable things, marry a Harvard man!

MONTY WOOLLEY: From my first days at Yale, I selected companions who played pianos and felt it was no disgrace to read books not on the required reading list. It would be an understatement to say that other Yalemen distrusted us, in spite of the fact that one of its own, Cole Porter, gave them their best and most memorable football songs, "Bull Dog" and "Bingo Eli Yale."

GERALD MURPHY: "There was this barbaric custom of going around to the rooms of sophomores and talking with them to see which ones would be right material for the fraternities. I remember going around and seeing, several nights running, a sign on one boy's door: "Back at ten P.M., gone to football song practice." Gordon Hamilton, the handsomest and most sophisticated boy in the class, was enormously irritated that anyone would have the gall to be out of his room on visiting night and decided not to call on him after all. But one night I was passing the room and went in, just to say hello. There was a single electric bulb in the center of the ceiling, wicker furniture, which was considered a bad sign at Yale in 1911, a piano with a box of caramels (sent by his mother from Arnold's Candies, Peru, Indiana; today the shop still makes those same caramels and the famous "Cole Porter Fudge") and a little dark man with his hair parted in the middle and slicked down, wearing a salmon-pink tie and a checked suit, looking like a Westerner dressed for the East. We had a long talk about music and composers, discovering that we were both crazy about Gilbert and Sullivan.

EDDIE WITTSTEIN: Cole was a good pianist, and though not an especially talented singer, he was excellent at putting over his own lyrics. I always liked him and played a lot of his football songs at the dining hall and the Yale proms.

New Haven Register (**November 12, 1911**):   COLE PORTER, LATEST COMPOSER OF BIG CHORUSES, LOOKS TO NEW HITS "BULL DOG" AND "ELI" TO CHEER TEAM TO VICTORY NEXT WEEK.

ARNOLD WHITRIDGE: I much preferred his early songs, such as "A Tale of the Oyster," "You Don't Know Paree," and "Poor Young Millionaire." The later songs are too arty, too metallic. In the post-Yale years, from far-flung outposts around the globe, Cole would greet Yale friends and classmates, wildly reminiscing about those glorious college years.

After we left college we saw very little of each other, but when we did meet we picked up just where we left off. It just happened that our paths lay in different directions.

It was only at the end of his life when Cole was a very sick man that he and I came close to each other again. He was in bad shape then and could not play the piano anymore. He used to ask my wife and myself to supper sometimes and I would sing one of his old songs ("I've a Shooting Box in Scotland," "We're a Group of Nonentities" and "She Was a Fair Young Mermaid") to him that he had long forgotten. After I got through he would say, "Did I write that?" "You certainly did," I answered, and he would say, "It's not bad, is it?" It was very touching to me— just before the end of his life.

Cole Porter and his second banana, Monty Woolley, were full of pranks and practical jokes, perpetrated upon each other and their fellow students. Monty Woolley recalled an insight into the mirthful side of life at Yale, circa 1910–1913.

MONTY WOOLLEY: One time we sent out invitations to two dozen or so socially acceptable undergraduates. The elaborately engraved invitations, complete with a coronet and three plumes, commanded the students to appear at an inn outside New Haven to meet Edward, Prince of Wales, and assigned each guest the name of a member of the British Peerage, with explicit instructions to wear the exact costume and decorations assigned to the rank of each of the actual noblemen.

We hired open carriages to convey our guests to the inn and footmen in full regalia plied the youths with the finest vintage champagne. There, awaiting the Yalemen at the inn was His Royal Highness, impersonated by Cole Porter in black satin knee breeches, complete with the Order of the Garter blazing on his velvet lapel.

I played the role of the Court Chamberlain, presented each of the guests to the Prince in order of hierarchy. And once our ruse was discovered, Cole sat down at the inn's piano and regaled our guests with contemporary college songs, many of them composed by him, in a very unprincely manner.

OF THE THREE hundred songs Cole wrote while at Yale, many were sprinkled throughout the productions of the Yale Dramatic Association and played and sung during the Christmas tours of the Glee Club. Cole especially received favorite-son treatment from Yale alumni everywhere; audiences went wild over his act, and reviewers spoke glowingly of his performances, one saying, "Cole Porter '13 can secure a place on the Orpheum program when he is so inclined. 'A Football King' is entirely his own idea, and when he and the club had finished it, he sat down to the piano and one after another responded with three or four encores. His recitative work is clever."

All these comments and press clippings were sent off to Kate, and she rushed them to the local press in Peru, where they got front-page treatment. Kate had molded this only son well, creating a true campus boulevardier and setting him on a course that would set the musical world on fire. Her scrapbooks overflowed with press clippings and memorabilia of every sort connected with her son's meteoric rise in the Yale social firmament.

Cole Porter's efforts while at Yale were not entirely devoted to composing songs. He occasionally put pen to a literary effort, as he would do throughout his life. The following vignette, written to celebrate the first anniversary of the Taft Hotel in downtown New Haven, was delivered at Scroll and Key, the secret senior society and the most social, on January 16, 1913:

COLE PORTER: It seems only fitting when the Taft Hotel is about to celebrate its first birthday to immortalize the celebration by writing an essay on "The New Hotel of America."

Of course, every town in the country with a sense of decency has a new hotel these days. You may travel to the little city and look for the shabby hotel whose plush parlors you used to dread, only to find instead a wonderful skyscraper on the main street making all the early Victorian shops about it fairly black with rage.

The minute you arrive, the native who meets you begins booming the hotel to the skies. You are told with hushed awe of the interior decoration, and of the vulgar display of bathrooms. Then after leading up gradually, he ends up giving you the prize package—he mentions the grill—for there is always a grill. This is perhaps the most typical feature of the New Hotel, the grill is a low-ceilinged, rottingly ventilated cellar where the piece de resistance is rarebit, where the vintage is Budweiser, all of which is accompanied by an orchestra from Long Branch taking the name of Robert E. Lee in vain.

With the coming of the new type of hotel, we have lost the dear old American plan, the famous gorge, the delight of the really hungry, which required no imagination to satisfy the appetite. Do you remember the days when a heavily be-trayed waiter used to place your plate on the table and then encircle it with little bathtubs, the whole giving the impression of a sun surrounded by a myriad of satellites? And will you ever forget the old menu that reveled in its number of vegetables, and gloated over its variety of pie?

But those have passed now, and in its stead, we are present-ed with an aesthetic European plan menu wearing a cover on which is painted a lady in an impossible decollete gown rising out of a glass of champagne.

But these abuses which beset us are as nothing compared with the architectural evil in the typical New Hotel. And of course, New York is blamed again, when really the whole trouble lies with the owners of the hotels in our little towns. Every little village hotel owner decided to imitate the innocent metropolis to a T. As a result of this we see such a spectacle as the Hotel Taft which completely demoralizes the effect of a New England college campus.

But we rejoice to say that our American taste shows signs of improvement. This is a new era of hotels in America. Perhaps in a few years we shall return as graduates and refer to the dear old days when the Taft stood there.

"The New Hotel of America" provides an insight into Cole's continued preoccupation with wordplay. The essay is also interesting in light of Cole's developing fascination with hotels.

AS GRADUATION NEARED, Kate Porter, having given in to her father's insistence that Cole attend Harvard Law School, managed to extract from J.O. a summer trip for Cole to England as a graduation gift. There he explored the glories of the English countryside with classmates Peter Cooper Bryce, Charles Marshall, and Gurney Smith. The joys of an English summer and the thoughts of the coming year at Harvard precluded Cole from giving too much thought to the future.

Members of the graduating class had given Cole Porter the fifth-largest number of votes as the person who had done the most for Yale. He was voted the most entertaining, the second-most original (losing to Ewing T. Webb by five votes), and the most eccentric. The latter accolade certainly covered a multitude of behavioral patterns and today would have been far more explicit, possibly sounding a humorous note on Cole Porter's life-style.

A survey of the 292 graduates of the Class of 1913 also revealed that Cole was one of the 128 who used alcohol, one of 178 who smoked, one of 69 non-church members, and one of 110 who had been abroad.

In addition to the three hundred songs, Cole Porter's legacy at Yale consisted of six musical productions written for fraternity "smokers" and the Yale Dramat: *Cora* (1911), *And the Villain*

Still Pursued Her (1912), *The Pot of Gold* (1912), *The Kaleidoscope* (1913), *Paranoia* (1914) and *We're All Dressed Up and We Don't Know Huerto Go* (1914).

MONTY WOOLLEY: I introduced Cole to the theater. From his very first days at Yale we developed a friendship, and my instincts told me, here is a future genius who only needs the proper direction to sharpen his already budding talent.

We often stayed at my father's hotel, the Marie Antoinette on Broadway. The usual procedure was for me to steal a passkey from a less than dutiful desk clerk and then proceed to an elegant unoccupied suite. It was our habit to order the most expensive vintage champagne and turn the entire evening into a Yale reunion. More often than not my father was informed and when that would happen, he would arrive, give us a stiff reprimand, threaten to cut off my monthly allowance and then toss us all back into the street.

COLE ACCEDED RELUCTANTLY to his grandfather's wishes and entered Harvard Law School in September 1913. Through the first semester he gave a halfhearted try at "Civil Procedure at Common Law," "Criminal Law and Procedure," and "Property and Torts"—courses faced by all first-year law students. But his mind just did not have a legal bend, and his heart as well as his mind was with his music.

With his roommate at Craigie Hall, T. Lawrason Riggs (Yale, 1910), Cole turned his attention to the annual "smoker" show he had promised the Yale Dramatic Association. This production, *We're All Dressed Up and Don't Know Huerto Go*, was a farce based loosely on the Mexican revolution and proved to be every bit as silly and successful as Cole's other shows for Yale.

This aspect of Cole's first year at Harvard was kept well under wraps from J.O.; Kate, however, was well informed of her son's continuing theatrical efforts.

Just before Cole's second year, the dean of Harvard Law School, Ezra Ripley Thayer (who had seen Cole performing at a Harvard smoker) prodded him to switch to the Harvard Graduate School of Arts and Sciences. He was to major in music, enrolling in only two courses—one in basic harmony and the other in music appreciation. This allowed him ample time to run down to New Haven and New York. All of this was done with the full indulgence of Kate but again J.O. was not informed.

Cole again did not apply himself and he seems to have just drifted through this year at the Graduate School of Arts and Sciences. It can be assumed that most of Cole's time was devoted to composing songs and indulging his growing taste for life in New York, where he frequently joined Monty Woolley and former Yale classmate Leonard Hanna on Broadway's first-night circuit.

COLE ABANDONED HIS graduate studies and Harvard's loss became Broadway's gain. He took up residence at the Yale Club in New York and continued to broaden his circle of wealthy and influential friends. As things turned out, even Cole's first big effort on broadway was a product of the social world in which he moved. One prominent figure he met was Elizabeth "Bessie" Marbury, who knew everybody and doubled as a theatrical producer and literary agent. Through her, Cole met the elite of Broadway as well as the international social set, and because of these connections his songs were used in a number of Broadway productions of the day.

Bessie Marbury was a hopelessly plain lesbian who tended toward stoutness and wore her straight, brown hair in a tight knot on top of her head. For forty-five years, she was the lover of internationally famed interior decorator Elsie de Wolfe. Eventually, she left Elsie for the much-younger Anne Morgan, daughter of financier J. P. Morgan. Later in life, she became a powerhouse in the Democratic Party and a friend of First Lady Eleanor Roosevelt, Governor Al Smith, and Mayor Jimmy Walker. Under Miss Marbury's urging, Cole and classmate T. Lawrason Riggs immersed themselves in the creation of an American comic opera following in the tradition of Gilbert and Sullivan.

Cole displayed an early talent as a phrasemaker by contributing the title, *See America First.* The entire show was a spoof of the flag-waving musicals made popular by George M. Cohan, and combined cowboys and Indians, wealthy politicians, and a rebellious suffragette daughter.

Things went wrong from the very beginning. The entire production mirrored Bessie Marbury's social background and gave scant consideration to making the show a professional and financial success. For one thing, Bessie Marbury made the error of casting one of Elsa Maxwell's "young things," Dorothie Bigelow, as the daughter. Miss Bigelow, equipped with a heavy British pedigree and no theatrical experience, could not even project her voice beyond the third row during rehearsal at the small Maxine Elliott Theatre. But Cole remained undaunted, for he was about to have his name on a Broadway show.

Unfortunately, no amount of rehearsing, doctoring, or infusion of new tunes could save *See America First.* It opened on March 27, 1916, to a glittering society audience (rounded up by Bessie Marbury). The critics roasted the show.

The New York Tribune: Gotham is a big town and it may be that the sisters, aunts and cousins of its Yalemen will be sufficient to guarantee prosperity for *See America First.* That is its best chance.

Charles Darton/*Evening World:* Whatever else may be said of *See America First,* on view last night at Maxine Elliott's Theatre, it must be granted that T. Lawrason Riggs and Cole Porter did everything in their power to follow the earlier example set by Gilbert and Sullivan . . . but they have achieved nothing more than college boys might have done in the way of entertainment.

New York American: A high-class college show played partly by professionals might be a fair description of the musical comedy, *See America First.*

The demise of *See America First* had some positive results for Cole and the others connected with the show. G. Schirmer published thirteen of the show's songs, including the title tune and three numbers originally written for *Paranoia*: "I've a Shooting Box in Scotland," "Prithee Come Crusading With Me," and "Lady Fair, Lady Fair." Of the published numbers, "I've a Shooting Box in Scotland" was recorded by Victor, in 1916, by the Joseph C. Smith Orchestra. It was the first commercial recording of a Cole Porter tune, and Cole always referred to it as "Shooting Pains in Scotland."

Others from the unlamented show did well. Walter Wanger, a Dartmouth man who served the show as a production assistant, went on to fame and fortune as a Hollywood movie producer. Clifton Webb became a well-known song-and-dance man on Broadway and then went on to greater glory in the movie industry.

The year 1916 also brought Cole good tidings from home (a place he rarely mentioned). On December 16, 1916, J. O. Cole set up a trust for Cole to receive a substantial income from J.O.'s numerous holdings in farming land, coal and gas, and lumber properties after the death of J.O. and his partner, Clifton Crane. As both partners were in their eighties, Cole could look forward to financial independence somewhere in the near future.

After the demise of *See America First,* Cole claims to have gone into hiding, but actually he was living at the Yale Club in New

York and was very visible at society gatherings and the theater almost every night.

Then in July 1917, he decided on the spur of the moment to set out for war-ravaged Europe. (Throughout his life, he would make travel plans almost on a moment's notice. Monty Woolley told me of the time he and Cole passed a steamship office and Cole stepped in and requested passage on the next available ship.) Cole boarded the ship with a portable zither strapped jauntily on his back, an instrument that had been given to him by Charlie Munn (a major stockholder in Lyon & Healy, the Chicago music firm). It had a piano keyboard about two and a half feet wide and looked very much like a miniature baby grand piano with collapsible legs.

It was not so much a case of an innocent abroad as it was a case of innocence long since abandoned; Cole was a young American sybarite seeking to be anointed by his peers at what was then the citadel of the civilized world—Paris.

3

"Anything Goes"

THE PARIS COLONY that welcomed Cole Porter, even in the middle of World War I, had a very active homosexual colony with an ample sprinkling of bisexuals, transvestites, and male and female impersonators. And the French capital catered to all their needs, both cultural and sexual.

Prominent lesbian couples influenced the arts and theatrical world. Gertrude Stein and Alice B. Toklas, Elsie de Wolfe, and Bessie Marbury held court at Versailles with two other moneyed American women: Anne Morgan and Anne Vanderbilt (second wife of William Kissam Vanderbilt and stepmother to Consuelo, Duchess of Marborough).

Cole developed a long-standing friendship with a married couple, Prince and Princess Edmond de Polignac. She was the former Winnaretta Singer, the eldest daughter of the sewing machine magnate Isaac Singer. In addition to devoting her considerable fortune to a variety of artistic, scientific, and social causes, she tolerated her husband's sole diversion in life—pursuing handsome young men with theatrical ambitions. The Prince and Princess de Polignac not only opened to Cole Porter the world of Faure, Ravel, Satie, Stravinsky, and Milhaud, but also saw to it that the doors of every salon in the Fauborg St. Germain swung open to the yet-unheralded American composer.

Cole's war record has never really been documented. He maintained that he joined the French Foreign Legion as a private, transferred to the Ecole d'Artillerie at Fontainebleau, and saw service at the front with the 32nd Regiment, French Army.

The Yale Class of 1913, in an annual devoted to the war activities of its members, adds to the confusion of his war record with the comment that "Classmate Cole A. Porter has joined the American Aviation Forces in France although nobody seems to know in what capacity." Further muddling the truth was Cole's fabricated story that France awarded him the Croix de Guerre.

MONTY WOOLLEY: Porter had more changes than Marechal Foch. And wore them with a complete disregard of regulations. One night he might be a captain of the Zouaves, the next an aide-de-camp.

COLE PORTER: (Letter to his mother, which she promptly sent on to *The Peru Republican* for publication, appearing October 5, 1917.)

Dear Mother: An awfully cheery letter arrived from you today (September 4) dated August 13.

Life here continues to offer great surprises. For instance, yesterday I went to inspect the village of Fresnoy. As I was walking along the road of the town I passed the entrance of an abri (shelter in case of air raids). But it looked so much better than most of them that I opened the door to it. I peered down the steps (they are usually about twenty feet below the surface) and there, at the bottom stood a woman of about sixty years smiling up at me. She asked me to come down, which

I did, and found an immaculately clean room, a dirt floor swept to a polish, and this was her home. She told me her story—how she was all alone in the world, her husband and son having been killed, but until the Boches had come, she had lived in her brick house, on her farm, with thirty cows (she had prizes for cattle on her walls in the cave). Then, the invasion. She fled, but was taken prisoner, sent to Prussia to work, grew ill and was returned to France by way of Switzerland, went back to her home at Fresnoy, found it had completely disappeared, and she happened on this German abri as the only shelter she could find. Of course it was an astounding adventure she'd had, but the amazing part was her gaiety and her charm. I love this French race. They're so attractive, so amusing, so wonderfully brave, and so simple—just like children, all of them. So, we being without a cook, and being tired of opening canned beans, asked her if she could cook. And she said, "Oh, Monsieur, of course I can cook." So I said, "Pack up your things and jump in the motor." So here she is, this extraordinary old sport, living in the house with us, working like a Trojan, and cooking delicious omelettes, rabbit chops and compotes. And she has forgotten her troubles and we've forgotten ours.

Last night being very clear and calm, I went to the aviation camp with the commandant of this canton, to see a glimpse at least of the only attractively exciting side of the whole war. I stood there and saw sixty aeroplanes rise, one by one, and make for St. Quentin. Before each aviator mounted his plane he would come up to his captain, shake his hand, and cry, "Au revoir, mon Capitaine!" and run off to his job. It was very touching, Mother, to see all this and to know that nearly every night one of these aeroplanes either never returns or else falls and kills its occupants.

A little later we saw three German caterpillars. The caterpillar is the newest German atrocity. It consists of a string of burning torches which is shot from the ground. It rises quickly and if it hits the French aeroplane it wraps itself about it and burns the plane and the occupants in the air. The French are completely "up in the air" about it. They fear it as nothing else and they can't understand how it is made.

I spent today in Erchen, and tomorrow I go to Amiens. I'm gradually getting awfully well-acquainted with this country in the zone-des-armees, and I've worked hard over my Ford camion that it runs perfectly. I know "Sammie" will be glad to hear that I really am developing into quite a mechanic.

A letter from headquarters today says that the reports from the French officers here in charge were pleased with the thoroughness and the speed of my inspections. I've interviewed over one thousand people and on finishing up here they want me to take charge of an inspection tour of the Vosges Mountains.

Arnold Whitridge is a captain of Gen. Pershing's staff. I have seen him.

I am so glad that your garden has been such a success. I can see you eating those delicious things now. Oh, I'd love to run out to Westleigh for about two weeks and then bring you back to France with me. I like my job and my health was never better.

Lots of love to all of you.

Affectionately,
COLE

Roye-sur-Somme
September 4, 1917

THE SINGLE MOST important person that Cole met in wartime Paris was Linda Lee Thomas, an alimony millionairess from Louisville, Kentucky, late of New York and Newport, and ten years older than Cole. She was a great southern beauty who, while not a bartered bride, was certainly a mentally battered one who was granted a $1 million settlement from newspaper heir Edward R. Thomas *(New York Morning Telegram)* for all her troubles.

Cole and Linda met at the Hotel Ritz wedding reception of Ethel Harriman and Henry Russell, January 30, 1918.

SCHUYLER LIVINGSTON PARSONS: The next day Linda Thomas called me up and asked who the man and girl were who played so well at the wedding, begging me to bring them to dinner with her and have them perform. I said I would try, that they were friends of mine, Cole Porter and Mimi Scott. I asked them but I guess I wasn't very tactful, for they took offense and asked if Linda thought they were public entertainers. After a while I pacified them and they accepted. The night came and I stopped for them at Mimi's apartment where they kept me waiting a long time. I was annoyed at the delay and furious when they appeared made up as music-hall performers of the Toulouse-Lautrec period, Mimi in a jet dress and picture hat, Cole in a dreadful tail coat with high collar and with his hair slicked down. "Now," they said, "this will put you and your swell friends in their place." By the time we arrived at Linda's they had lost some of their bravado; when I dashed upstairs and told [Linda] what a ghastly trick they had played, she roared, as did her guests, and even I cooled down enough to be able to introduce them as they made their grand entrance. It was a most successful party and not a year later Cole and Linda were married.

The Paris Herald (December 19, 1919): The marriage of Mr. Cole Porter of Peru, Indiana, who saw service in the French Army during the war, and Mrs. Lee Thomas of Louisville, Kentucky, was celebrated yesterday at the Mairie of the Eighteenth Arrondissement. After a brief visit in the south of France, Mr. and Mrs. Porter will make their home in Paris.

Boy with one million weds Girl with two million.

Although the wedding ceremony was short and simple, the honeymoon actually extended beyond France into Italy via a private railway car and a slew of servants.

The Porters set up housekeeping at Linda's house at 13 rue Monsieur in the fashionable Quartier des Invalides. Thanks to Linda's great taste, the interior was an Art Deco symphony: zebra rugs on highly polished marble floors, red lacquered chairs with cushions covered in white kidskin, settees covered in suede, platinum-colored wallpaper, and a huge basement room entirely lined with mirrors and used solely for dancing and parties.

BROOKE ASTOR: I knew Cole after I married Buddie.... When we went on our honeymoon trip in 1928, we went often to the rue Monsieur for dinner. It was such a charming house, decorated to perfection.

This was my first exposure to Linda Lee Porter. I did not know her well, I don't think anybody did, really. Linda was one of those people with innate taste; she had taste in everything— houses, beautiful furniture, decorative objects, and she served beautifully, all done effortlessly. She had total elegance! Some people who collect have beautiful furniture but have terrible taste in clothes.

Linda was not stuffy, if she knew you. Because she was so worldly she taught him a lot. He could never have written the type of songs he wrote without her. She launched him into that set. The chic world. It was not the fast lane, it was the chic, intercontinental, European set. That is how and when it all began.

ELSA MAXWELL: I felt antagonistic toward him. I thought he was trying to be excessively cute, and I've always been allergic to that approach in men and women, adults and children. Further, he was dressed too immaculately for a young composer who had been roasted by the critics. I had seen too many gigolos in Europe to be taken in by fine feathers. I pegged him for a phony, easily the worst snap judgment I made in my first seventy years.

"You must be flat broke or you wouldn't dress so well," I said rudely in my annoyance. Cole waved airily, "All on tick, Grandpa's tick."* I saw that he was tight and that, too, rubbed me the wrong way. I've never been able to tolerate people who drink too much, although I must confess that Cole made a large dent in that prejudice in my later years.

The fact that Linda Lee Thomas Porter chose a practicing homosexual as her second husband has led to much speculation as to whether Linda herself was a lesbian. Her climb up the social ladder was aided by her long-standing friend, Elsie de Wolfe, an avowed lesbian, and later in life she struck up a close bond with the Imperial Russian princess Natasha Paley Wilson, another member of the international lesbian and male homosexual community. While this indicates that Linda and her circle looked the other way when it came to the morals of others—just so long as they had wealth or social position or, better yet, equal amounts of both—I have found nothing to document the rumors that Linda may have had lesbian tendencies.

Her divorce from newspaper heir Edward Russell Thomas could have turned into a scandal, but Linda was silenced by her mother-in-law with the $1 million settlement. The dark

---

*Cole was then receiving $100 a month from J. O. Cole, cut from the $500 a month he received while at Yale.

side of that marriage never hit the headlines, but it was a well-known fact among Linda's friends that Ned Thomas was a philanderer, alcoholic, and woman-beater. Whether he beat Linda or not cannot be verified; however, she endured enough mental suffering to seek a divorce and the prominent Thomas family, fearing a scandal, paid her off rather than see Ned Thomas's sordid affairs paraded before the public.

Her marriage to the much younger* Cole Porter was a refuge, a marriage that would make few demands on her and absolutely no demands sexually. At first she saw herself more his patron than his wife, someone who could use her new fortune and social connections to enable Cole Porter to take a more solid position in the world that had been his goal since he first arrived East from Peru, Indiana. In time, his celebrity would become so great that he would overshadow any celebrity acquired from her beauty and wealth.

MICHAEL ARLEN: Every morning at half past seven, Cole Porter would leap lightly out of bed and, having said his prayers, arrange himself in a riding habit. Then, having written a song or two, he appeared at the stroke of half past twelve at the Ritz, where leaning manfully on the bar, he would say, "Champagne cocktail, please. Had a marvelous ride this morning!" That statement gave him strength and confidence by which to suffer this, our life, until ten minutes past three in the afternoon, when he would fall into a childlike sleep.

ALFRED DE LIAGRE, JR.: I first met Cole Porter in the summer of 1926 when Monty Woolley brought me for dinner to this charming house in the rue Monsieur; the house and the Port-

*One source claimed that Linda was actually fourteen years Cole's senior and not the ten years generally reported.

54

ers' life-style were both remarkable, especially in the eyes of a Yale undergraduate.

For the next three weeks we met almost every noon at the Ritz bar for champagne cocktails, the required beverage of all expatriates in Paris in the mid-twenties. Cole generally had as guests at his table one or two of the following: Philip Barry, Archibald MacLeish, Robert Chanler, Prince Michael Romanoff, Groucho Marx, or Scott Fitzgerald.

MOSS HART: I dined twice with the Porters during my ten-day stay in Paris and fell in love, as everybody did, with Linda Porter. To fall in love with Linda Porter was as much a part of a young man's first trip to Paris as eating snails at Fouquet's or climbing the Eiffel Tower. They were rich, they were gifted, and they moved about with infinite ease and light-heartedness in two worlds—the world of fashion and glitter and the pantaloon world of theater. Their house in Paris was exquisite, one of the most beautiful homes I have ever seen, and Linda Porter, a legendary beauty herself, lent something of her own radiance and splendor to their life together so that everything and everyone in their house seemed to shine and sparkle with a little of her own special grace. She was a woman of immense delicacy, with an enchanting turn of mind, as easily beguiled by a chorus girl as a duchess and equally at home with both.

COLE AND LINDA returned to the United States in 1923, and were living at 735 Fifth Avenue in New York when on February 3, word arrived from Peru, Indiana, that family patriarch J. O. Cole had died at age eighty-five. In addition to the Cole-Crane trust, the estate consisted of $1 million in cash. Kate shared her $500,000 cash bequest with Cole, who then proceeded to head right back to Europe with Linda and his newfound wealth. For the first time in his entire life, he was independently wealthy.

The Coleporteurs (as they were known to Le Tout Paris)

flirted briefly with the Riviera, following Gerald and Sara Murphy to the south of France. They rented La Garoupe, a large villa near Cap d'Antibes, but the urbane Porters quickly became bored with the then-pastoral setting of the place. They did not return the next season.

Their next stop was Venice, where for successive seasons, they rented the Palazzo Barbaro, the Papadopoli, and the Palazzo Rezzonico, where Lord Byron lived and Robert Browning died.

DIANA VREELAND: I want to tell you two things about Cole Porter.

The first has to do with that wonderful house of his at 13 rue Monsieur. When you rang the bell at number 13, the concierge would open the door and let you in and there you would look through into an apple orchard, and in the apple orchard stood a half-timbered Normandy farmhouse. This was the house of Cole and Linda Porter when they lived in Paris. The house was filled with the most beautiful objects and furniture, paintings and drawings, carpets, porcelain and linens, marvelous food, and wonderful sounds—Cole's piano.

The other story is on Venice. At daybreak, while half of Venice slept, Cole would be out in his gondola, taking instruction from his gondolier. The gondolier would be sitting in the seat where Cole normally sat, shouting orders up to Cole. Cole would be back in the stern of the boat, singing at the top of his lungs, and the little ribbons on his gondolier hat would be fluttering in the morning breeze, as he was absorbing his lesson in gondoliering and learning the beat of the oar.

Cole and Linda were launched on the Venetian scene by American-born Princess Jane di San Faustino,* née Jane

*Princess di San Faustino is grandmother to Fiat chairman Gianni Agnelli.

Campbell of New Jersey. In the Venice of the 1920s, she was regarded as the first and last word on who was "In" and who was "Out."

Once launched, the Porters set about giving a dazzling series of grand parties in their rented Venetian palaces. The most memorable, the "Red and White Ball," was held at the Palazzo Rezzonico. Fifty handsome, muscular gondoliers, dressed as statuesque footmen, lined the stairway, with lighted torches in hand, as three hundred guests entered the palazzo from the Porter's private dock on the Grand Canal.

Carrying out the party's color motif, the Porters had specially made red-and-white paper costumes representing four distinct periods in nineteenth-century Venetian life and distributed them to their guests. Colored lights and 250,000 candles played on the ballroom, as acrobats swayed above the canal on a tightrope. Among those present were Elsa Maxwell, Monty Woolley, Billy Reardon, Lady Diana Duff Cooper, Howard Sturges, Marchese di Portago, Baron de Gunsburg, Countess di Frasso, Sir Charles and Lady Mendl, and Prince Frederick Leopold of Prussia.

FANNY BRICE: From Cannes we went to Venice and Cole Porter has this big palazzo, I do not know how many rooms. I'll bet five thousand people could dance in the ballroom.

We are at the Lido, at the beach, and Cole is getting a little bored, and he says, "Come on back to the house, Fanny, I'm going to write some songs for you."

We went to the ballroom in this palazzo and there was a piano at each end of it. And all those paintings of the families who had lived in this palazzo. Cole and I are at one end of this big ballroom, sitting at the piano. And he gets an idea for a song to be done with a Jewish accent. All of a sudden I look up and see this little guy at the piano and me with him, in this big ballroom where God knows who had lived, and he's trying to write me a little Jewish song. I just couldn't get over it. I guess I broke the mood, and I never did get that song.

COLE PORTER (1953 LETTER TO ENTERTAINER GEORGE BYRON): Fanny Brice visited Venice in 1926, when my wife and I were living in the Palazzo Rezzonico. At this time in my life I had given up all hope of ever being successful on Broadway and had taken up painting, but Fanny, whom we grew to know very well, asked me to write a song for her. This was the reason for "Hot-House Rose." When I finished it, I invited her to the Rezzonico to hear it and afterwards she always told friends how wonderfully incongruous it was, that I should have demonstrated to her this song about a poor little factory girl as she sat beside me while I sang and played it to her on a grand piano that looked lost in our ballroom, whose walls were entirely decorated by Tiepolo paintings and was so big that if we gave a ball for less than a thousand people they seemed entirely lost. She never sang the song.

ROBERT KIMBALL: "Weren't We Fools?" was written for Fanny Brice and performed by her during her vaudeville act at New York's Palace Theatre beginning November 21, 1927. On the second night of the famous singing comedienne's week-long engagement, she learned that her former husband, Nicky Arnstein, was in the audience and so she dropped the tune for that evening's performance. Porter told a reporter for the *New York Telegram* that the song had been composed long before Miss Brice's sensational divorce from Arnstein.

ROSIE DOLLY: I visited Cole Porter often with my sister Jennie, during his Venetian years. We usually arrived with Gordon Selfridge aboard his yacht.

Gordon offered Cole an enormous sum of money if he would write an entire revue starring the Dolly Sisters. The idea

58

intrigued the then-struggling songwriter but nothing ever came of it.

SARA MURPHY: Cole was a natural-born hedonist, which is fine. People like hedonists. But Cole had so much more. He always liked beautiful, expensive things. Not that he thought about money, he never noticed it. He thought everyone had it because he never had to bother. But he wanted to live like a king, which is all right too, unless it stops you from working. That's what we were afraid of.

Of course, he wanted to marry a beautiful woman, which he did. Even I have to admit that. She was dull as anything, but she was very beautiful. Gerald and I always found her stuffy. Cole was such an affectionate, lovely man. We loved to go out with him alone. He was so bright and witty. If Linda came along, it made for sort of heavy going. Some people are like that. Partly it was her great beauty. She was so aware of it. She never moved her mouth, or made any false gestures that might cause her to develop a line in her face. Oh my, no! But Cole thought she was just wonderful, which was a very good thing if he was going to insist upon marrying her.

BROOKE ASTOR: Cole and Linda, you know, were not a terribly devoted couple for a long time. Her age, you know. He admired her. She gave him something he had not had up to that time. All those parties in Venice and all that sort of thing. Cole adored that type of life, he loved all the excitement and the fun of it. She liked it, too, but I really think that Linda enjoyed being in the background.

People like Buddie and Arnold liked him so much. Buddie was such an extraordinary man that when he found out that Cole was homosexual, he did not let it ruin their friendship. I don't think Averell was comfortable with it, but then after Yale he and Cole went their separate ways.

I must admit that I was a little nervous for a while when I saw them together. Then sensibly, I came to realize how Buddie felt about him. Cole had that other side to him. I don't think he really cared what people thought about him.

Newsweek (**May 18, 1953**): Porter is not himself a markedly effervescent man, but he likes to play host—he's naturally elegant; he is fond of festivity, and he has long been the kind of man who knows where the very special treat is to be obtained.

As one of his friends has said of Porter's early European years: "If there was a fine little hotel in Verona with just one table out of doors under an arbor, Cole would have heard of it."

SCHUYLER LIVINGSTON PARSONS: My biggest thrill of that winter was when Grover Loening asked me to put up Charles Lindbergh for a week or ten days . . . he suggested a Sunday lunch and a few men for dinner one night. I had no guest list for either, but I do know that there were musicians present since Lindbergh had said he liked music.

The men's party was handpicked by Grover Loening and I and was small enough so that everybody could really talk to the guest of honor. Cole Porter and George Gershwin outplayed themselves.

THE DUCHESS OF ALBA: My father and Cole Porter were very good and close friends. They traveled a lot together, not only throughout Spain but in America, Switzerland, and many other countries. It was in Granada at our palace, the Casa de Pilatos, that Cole Porter lived, especially enjoying the flamenco. Cole Porter once told me, "It was Spain and its flamenco which gave me, as they do to nearly every musician, the abiding influence with its regard to basic beats, changing tempos and pure melody and scale, at their purest and most primitive."

My memory of Cole Porter is not all that vivid, for I was very young at our first meeting. As a personal memory, I do remember one visit Cole made to our home. In those days I was just beginning to smoke, and as a gift, Mr. Porter gave me a beautiful Cartier cigarette holder. I do recall he came often to our mansions in Seville and Granada, both built before Columbus discovered America.

THE IDYLLIC VENETIAN period came to an abrupt end early in 1927. Monty Woolley never tired of recalling the many years of friendship he shared with Cole Porter, regaling friends and acquaintances alike with memories of the good times. I was fortunate enough to have been brought into that magic circle created by the witty and often caustic tongue of Monty Woolley, and during one of our late afternoon conversations in the bar of New York's Hotel Astor, he gave a detailed insight into the hasty departure of the Porters from Venice.

It seems a small tempest began brewing on the Grand Canal in 1926, when Cole Porter and a group of classy titled friends decided to float a nightclub on a barge. Tongues began to wag, none more viciously than that of the Russian ballet master, Serge Diaghilev. The racially prejudiced Diaghilev, according to Woolley, went into one of his famous tirades when he learned that Cole had hired Leslie (Hutch) Hutchinson and his all-black jazz band for the club. Hutch and his group were the rage of Paris, and it was quite a coup for Cole to have gotten them for his floating barge. Hutch was such a hit that even when the opening night on the barge ended in a gale, Cole kept Hutch and his men on to amuse and entertain all his friends for the entire season at the Palazzo Rezzonico.

Cole originally met Hutch, a legendary jazz musician, during those early days in Paris. According to Monty, Cole loved to recount to male friends that Hutch's talents went far beyond the keyboard; their affair lasted well into the early thirties.

Woolley profiled Hutch as a black Adonis both in appearance and reputation. A Jamaican by birth who arrived in Europe after World War I, he soon became an Olympian figure in the world of jazz with his good looks and musical talent and became a favorite of international society. According to Woolley, Hutch would sit at his highly polished concert grand Steinway with the lid up, dressed in white tie and tails, a large white handkerchief tucked up his sleeve. This handkerchief would frequently be drawn out in a carefully calculated gesture, Hutch using it to mop his sweat-beaded forehead after each number. Titled society women seeing this gesture went into near-hysteria.

Hutch sipped Perrier-Jouët Champagne from a Baccarat flute resting on the piano. (Woolley claimed that it was Hutch who first introduced Cole to the bubbly joy of Perrier-Jouët, and it remained Cole's favorite champagne for the rest of his life.) Hutch sang and played all Cole Porter, Noel Coward, George Gershwin and Vincent Youmans numbers, after learning them directly from the composers, and in later years Hutch's signature song, "Begin the Beguine," made him a fortune in recording royalties. Aside from his considerable skill at the piano, Hutch was recognized throughout Europe as a legendary stud, and his liaisons with a succession of celebrities, from Cole Porter to Edwina Mountbatten to Merle Oberon, made him as much in demand for his sexual prowess as for his music.

Whenever and wherever Hutch appeared, the room was filled with his legion of admirers from the world of society. Monty ended this particular anecdote by noting that, regardless of his audience, whenever Cole Porter entered a room where Hutch was playing, the great musician stopped whatever tune he was performing and immediately broke into a Cole Porter song. In part this was in gratitude for Cole making him a celebrity, and in part it was for all that wonderful music.

According to Woolley, when the Porters returned to Venice in mid-summer, 1927, they found in fact that the tempest of the previous summer had not died down. To the memory of that summer was added a series of rumors that began the minute Cole and Linda alighted from their private gondola. The rumors were fueled by parties Cole would give when Linda departed for health reasons to her retreat in the Swiss Alps. Woolley said that the parties often featured members of Italian nobility in high drag, and the blatant use of drugs.

Cole left Venice reluctantly, just before he would have been officially asked to depart. But leaving Venice had one salubrious effect—it made him resolve to return to the United States to find his future on Tin Pan Alley.

Just as Cole was recovering from his hasty retreat from Venice, he received word in Paris that his father, Samuel Fenwick Porter, had died at Westleigh Farms in Peru, on August 18, 1927. Sam Porter's death at age sixty-nine was attributed to complications following a nervous breakdown.

Cole immediately booked passage on the first ship out, but failed to reach Indiana in time for the funeral.

4

"Ridin' High"

RIDIN' HIGH, INDEED! This period of Cole Porter's life would see five productions to his credit in five years on the Broadway and West End skies.

As Cole Porter prepared to enter the decade of the thirties, he still had, at thirty-six, the darkly handsome good looks that made him a standout in the earlier Yale photographs. He was slightly built and boasted slicked-down jet black hair and dark brown eyes much like those of a lovable baby seal; he reminded one of a little boy in knee pants peeking under a circus tent—an image that he marketed most of his life.

He had blunt fingers and was the first to tell everybody that he did not have perfect pitch, yet the one constant throughout his long career was his enthusiasm for his music. Cole continued to study even after he became the toast of Broadway, discovering new styles and the characteristics of other composers, adapting this knowledge to many of his projects. He would never have less than a half-dozen musical irons in the fire at once.

He was delighted to be popular, all the more because his popularity arrived in such quick succession. What was surprising was that his urbane style—idiosyncratic and most difficult to play and sing—would become the most readily recognizable voice of the musical theater of the thirties. Score after score by Cole Porter came bursting forth like a Roman candle.

The words and music of Cole Porter songs rocketed about the Great White Way of the early thirties. Euphoria was just one of his specialties, and energy and pizzazz bubbled out of "Let's Do It, Let's Fall In Love," "You're The Top," "What Is This Thing Called Love?" and "The Tale of the Oyster."

These melodies, and others to follow, were far more revolutionary than anything else being done in America. Most of his melodies were overlaid with European rhythms, and his lyrics resembled the party people they were written for and about—smooth, brittle, and full of insinuations. To the majority of songwriters in America, "I love you" was still a simple declaration; to Cole Porter, cavorting among a diverse group of American expatriates, it was just a smart crack calling for a smart answer.

At first, Cole was not interested when his enthusiastic friends pressed him to publish these tunes. Since he had plenty of money, he was indifferent about making more.

COLE PORTER: Suppose I had to settle down on Broadway for three months just when I was planning to go to Antibes!

That was his attitude. Cole returned stateside only for his father's funeral before returning to his house in Paris. He was happily involved with the shining fleet of vicomtes, contessas, princes, and rich Americans that swept from London to Paris to Venice to the Riviera. The brash Elsa Maxwell was the tireless Tugboat Annie of Society who pulled them forever onward.

Cole's only ambition at the time was to be a gentleman composer who could move in the highest social circles instead of the back streets of Tin Pan Alley. Many of his contemporaries in the songwriting business considered him an "expatriate highbrow." The truth of the matter was that he was full of self-doubts, and his habitual traveling enabled him to vacillate—he didn't have to face the music. Time after time he turned down assignments, doubtful that he could create the necessary music for a given production.

Up to this point in his career, Cole Porter saw his music used incidentally in an occasional revue on both sides of the Atlantic: *Hitchy-Koo of 1919, Mayfair and Montmartre* (1922), *Hitchy-Koo of 1922, Within the Quota* (ballet, 1923), *Greenwich Village Follies* (1924), *Out O' Luck* (Yale Dramatic Society, 1925), and *La Revue des Ambassadeurs* (1928).

However, as America approached the closing years of the 1920s, having a song placed here and there in other people's productions was not what Cole Porter wanted. He now wanted to see his name on the marquee of a Broadway theater; he was ready to vindicate the failure of *See America First*.

His opportunity came when press agent Louis Shurr put him together with E. Ray Goetz, a flamboyant bon vivant entrepreneur. Goetz was putting together a show with Gallic flavor starring his wife, Irene Bordoni. When Richard Rogers and Lorenz Hart dropped out of the project, Shurr remembered Cole. Cole's Parisian background would prove to be invaluable in making *Paris* a hit.

TED FETTER: When I first met Cole, it was 1928, and I was a student in Eva La Gallienne's school that she ran in connection with something called the Civic Repertory Theatre in New York. One morning, possibly in October, this rather chipper voice said, "Is this Ted Fetter? I know who you are but you don't know who I am. I am a cousin of yours named Cole Porter." Well, he wasn't famous then but I did know who he was. "Sure, I've heard of you. You write songs." (He'd had some songs—"Old Fashioned Garden" had already been a hit, and he'd done *See America First,* which had one great song in it.) Anyhow, he said, "Well, I'm glad to meet you, we two members of our family who are in this crazy business."

And so he invited me to lunch at the old Ritz Hotel, which was around 44th Street and Madison, and I went up there and met him and he said, "I'm working on a new show called *Paris,* with Irene Bordoni in it. I'd love to play you some of my songs from it." So he played me the score. One song that I felt was one of the greatest ones was "Let's Do It," and that was replacing another song. Cole wrote most of the show, and of course "Let's Do It," particularly went through the roof.

And I was twenty-one or twenty-two, whatever it was, when you can do anything. I'll be a lyric writer, I love it, this is great. So I went home and wrote extra choruses of "Let's Do It" and showed them to him, and I said could I sell them as parodies to a nightclub singer and he said sure. So that was when I started to write lyrics in parody of Cole's songs. And then when he would get stuck sometimes, he would call me up and say, "Maybe you could suggest something," and that's what I did. I did it on several shows and he used some of them, and that's where I got the reputation for having written some of Cole Porter's songs, which is absolutely ridiculous.

Paris opened at New York's Music Box Theatre on October 8, 1928 and ran for 195 performances. Of the five Porter songs used, the clever "Let's Do It, Let's Fall In Love" was the most outstanding.

Robert Coleman/*New York Daily Mirror:* PARIS A MUSIC BOX HIT! "Let's Fall," a naughty ditty, will probably prove a first-rate success. . . .

Rowland Field/*The Brooklyn Times:* *Paris,* starring Irene Bordoni, is still another favored rendezvous at the Music Box. The singing and superior costumes of the star, "The Commanders" orchestra and Cole Porter songs with their smart lyrics are surely something to see and hear—if you can get in.

John J. Daily/*The Washington Post:* James J. Walker, the popular mayor of New York, occupied a box on opening night.

Richard Watts, Jr./*The New York Herald-Tribune:* French star sings Cole Porter's songs in sprightly farce put on at Music Box. The arrival of the popular Miss Irene Bordoni in her latest starring vehicle is of course always one of the events of the new season.

There were some of us at the Music Box last night, however, who had a suspicion that it was the absent Mr. Cole Porter who was the flaming star of the premiere of *Paris*.

Cole, expecting little at the hands of Broadway, had returned to his luxurious refuge in Paris. When the reviews reached him, he knew his problems were over. At the age of thirty-seven, with years of work and study behind him, Cole Porter could now be taken seriously as a songwriter. With this minor triumph in hand, it was inevitable that Cole would be back soon with brighter and better songs.

Following his success with *Paris*, he contributed his first work to a film. Two songs, "Here Comes the Bandwagon" and "They All Fall in Love," were included in the Paramount film, *The Battle of Paris*, released November 30, 1929. The film starred Cole's friend Gertrude Lawrence and Charles Ruggles.

COLE PORTER: My main inspiration for writing a song is a telephone call from a producer.

During his European sojourn, Cole Porter was engaged by British impresario Charles B. Cochran to do the score for *Wake*

Up and Dream. The show opened at the London Pavillion on March 5, 1929, and ran 263 performances. Cole included previously used tunes, such as "Looking at You" from *La Revue des Ambassadeurs* and "Let's Do It, Let's Fall in Love," from the still-running *Paris.* The big hit from *Wake Up and Dream* was "What Is This Thing Called Love?"

Liverpool Echo: The first night of *Wake Up and Dream* promises altogether to be one of the most brilliant in many years. Amongst the box and stall holders, I am told for the first night, will be: Mrs. Richard Guinness, Lady Colfax, Lord Furness, the Hon. John Jacob Astor, the Marquese de Casa Maura, the Marquess of Donegal, Lady Emerald Cunard, the Duke of Sutherland, Lady Diana Duff and Mr. Duff Cooper, and a host of other prominent people.

It was a typical Cole Porter audience, a following that he would maintain to the very end on both sides of the Atlantic.

The London Daily Mail: A number of pretty women, many of them American and French, added to the interest of the first night. They were friends of Mr. Cole Porter, the American writer responsible for so much of the revue, who spends so much of his time in France.

The Tattler: Last, but not least, there was Lady Cunard, who gave a supper party for Mr. Cole Porter after the performance. She collected all the most chic and beautiful women and the most handsome and clever men in London, a good start for a party! There was Lady Plunkett, Lady Stanley, Mrs. Evelyn Fitzgerald, Lady Curzon and Lady Victor Paget just to mention a few, while on the side of wit and learning ranked Lord Reading, Sir Thomas Beecham, Lord Gage, Lord Berners and many others. After delicious dishes of bacon and eggs and sausages (so typical of the American-born Emerald Cunard), Lady Cunard rapped on the table and called upon various members of the party, parliamentary and otherwise, to get up and perform.

The display of jewels was remarkable: Lady Mendl had a cluster of cabochon emeralds as large as a five-shilling piece on one of her bracelets and Mrs. Reggie Fellows wore the most lovely necklace of the same stone.

Wake Up and Dream arrived in New York, opening at the Selwyn Theatre, December 30, 1929, where it played for 136 performances. Except for Jack Buchanan replacing Sonnie Hale, the British cast remained intact. Tilly Losch* and Jessie Matthews became the talk of the town with their highly individual performances.

WALTER WINCHELL: The most whistley and contagious Cole Porter tune yet is named "What Is This Thing Called Love?" which is the outstanding feature if you ask us (and you probably will) of *Wake Up and Dream.*

Richard Watts, Jr./New York Herald-Tribune: A number of us who long have admired the lyrics of Cole Porter and wished that he would write a whole score without demonstrating his passion for zoology had our wish last night, but it hardly can be said that we were altogether satisfied. There is not one reference in *Wake Up and Dream* to the sex habits of the beaver and gnu, but on the other hand there is little of the brilliant style to be found in his better songs . . . "What Is This Thing Called Love?" is charming in every way but the rest of the score as

*Tilly Losch, a Viennese confection, later became the toast of London society as the wife of the Earl of Carnarvon, whose father discovered King Tut's tomb.

well as the remaining lyrics seemed last night interesting but less than striking.

The New Yorker: On opening night the audience was composed of well-dressed people who had paid a minimum of twenty-two dollars a seat and us badly-dressed pressmen who haven't paid a nickel for a seat since 1920. The house was, as we say in show business, "tough." My impression, and the impression of most of those present on that occasion, was that *Wake Up and Dream* was one of the dullest revues ever put on the local boards. . . .

There are numbers by Cole Porter which are among the best he has ever written ("Which Is the Right Life?", bandied about from show to show during the past two years, is something which should be included in any collection of twentieth-century masterpieces, although it may need Mr. Porter himself at the piano to sing it), and the whole smartness reflects great credit on its sponsors.

Brooks Atkinson/*The New York Times:***   Like the best feature of the revue, Cole Porter's lyrics and music are on the side of urbanity and taste and can join such words as "shy, unobtrusive, demure and elusive" and make sense.

NOW THAT *PARIS* and *Wake Up and Dream* were among his credits, Cole Porter accepted a new challenge: the opportunity to do his first complete score without a collaborator. It was something both friends and critics knew he could do, but up to this point Cole himself felt unprepared for the attempt. The show *Fifty Million Frenchmen* was also to become his first major hit. This effort, produced by the mercurial E. Ray Goetz and directed by the unflappable Monty Woolley, opened at the Lyric Theatre on November 27, 1929, and ran for 254 performances. The show starred William Gaxton, Genevieve Tobin,

Helen Broderick, and Betty Compton (the sweetheart of New York's racy Mayor Jimmy Walker).

Although twenty of Porter's songs were actually used in the show, he wrote almost twice that number for consideration. Among the tunes that were used were "You Do Something to Me," "Find Me a Primitive Man," "The Happy Heaven of Harlem," and "I Worship You." Goetz's lavish production complemented the best score Cole had done to date.

Brooks Atkinson/*The New York Times:* Meanwhile, the show dances along with enlivening rapidity. As the composer, Cole Porter has written pleasant tunes and excellent lyrics: a mauve Apache, entitled "Find Me a Primitive Man," which Evelyn Hoey sings with jaunty spirit; an amusing number, "Do You Want to See Paris?" staged with snap; "I'm In Love," which Genevieve Tobin sings well, and to which Ceballo's Hollywood Dancers, as they choose to call themselves, do a spectacular trick with black and white costumes.

Richard Watts, Jr./*New York Herald-Tribune:* Mr. Cole Porter continued his studies in natural history during the course of *Fifty Million Frenchmen*, which had its premiere last night.

WALTER WINCHELL: Oo-La-La! *Fifty Million Frenchmen* is a profane portrait of Paris, but a pippin, and it is distinguished by Cole Porter's score, a thoroughly contagious one!

The Albany News: MILLIONAIRE BUSY MAKING ANOTHER, AS THE WRITER OF SOPHISTICATED SONGS.

GENEVIEVE TOBIN: Cole Porter was unique; no one like him in the musical theater then or now. When he said no, it was no! When he said yes, it was yes! He was very definite about what he wanted out of song. From the first rehearsal of *Fifty Million*

Frenchmen, Cole told me not to push too hard, to let the words speak for themselves.

BROOKE ASTOR: He really did so much to enhance the lives of other people with his music. Cole added an awful lot to everybody's lives, especially the life of anybody who had any pep. He was so clever, so witty.

COLE AND LINDA returned to New York from an extended trip to the Orient and Europe in the summer of 1930, and he immediately began work with Herbert Fields and Ray Goetz on *The New Yorkers,* a show based on an idea developed by Goetz and *The New Yorker* magazine's cartoonist Peter Arno. Just as *Fifty Million Frenchmen* evolved into a musical tour of Paris, *The New Yorkers* became a tour with music of Manhattan. Monty Woolley was again called upon to direct. The show, which starred socialite Hope Williams, Jimmy Durante, Ann Pennington, Lou Clayton, Eddie Jackson, and Fred Waring and His Pennsylvanians, opened at The Broadway Theatre on December 8, 1930, and ran 168 performances.

The bittersweet "Love For Sale," was the show's most memorable tune. It also became Cole's all-time favorite. Many New York critics took exception to the song as "in the worst possible taste." Not long after that criticism, radio executives throughout the country banned the song from the airwaves.

Fortunately for Cole, despite (or because of) the radio censorship there were enough word-of-mouth reports about "Love For Sale" during the Broadway run that recordings of the song by Fred Waring and His Pennsylvanians and other top artists were in great demand. The furor surrounding the lyrics made it one of Cole's biggest hits.

Charles Darnton/*New York Evening World:*   "Love For Sale," as sung by Kathryn Crawford, June Shafer, Ida Pearson and Stella Friend, was in the worst possible taste. . . .

The New Yorker: I thought that Cole Porter's lyrics were this time more distinctive than his music, but as I seem temperamentally unable to judge a song's merits until I hear it played later by a dance orchestra or on a piano at home, I am saying nothing. It took me two weeks to catch on to the score of *Fifty Million Frenchmen.*

New York Sun: Cole Porter contributed music and lyrics of almost Cole Porter quality.

COLE PORTER: This song I had concocted one night while strolling the rainy streets of London. It was called "Love For Sale." It became one of my string of standard hits, but the lyrics and the subject matter banned it forever from the radio networks as a song. . . .

KATE PORTER: I wish Cole would change the words of his censored song, "Love For Sale." It's such a pretty tune and it's a shame they don't play it.

ROBERT KIMBALL: At the New York opening, "Love For Sale" was sung by Kathryn Crawford and the Three Girl Friends. Because of critical objections to the "taste" of the song, the authors changed the scene in which it was presented from "In front of Reuben's" to the "Cotton Club, Lenox Avenue, Harlem," and the singer to a "colored girl."*

It was with this show that Linda Porter began the tradition of presenting to Cole the famous cigarette boxes and cases especially created to commemorate the opening of a specific show. For *The New Yorkers* opening, she commissioned Cartier to design a gold and silver case with a crossed reed motif. Its oval

*Elisabeth Welch took over as solo singer and did the song in the new setting.

end panels opened to reveal match compartments, and inside the lid was engraved, *"The New Yorkers,* December 8, 1930."

THE DEPRESSION-LADEN thirties were far removed from the sophisticated world of Cole Porter, and as the decade rolled on his fame as a composer spread.

FRED ASTAIRE: When I heard Cole Porter had agreed to do the score [for *Gay Divorce*], I signed the contract.

Cole had an especially difficult time writing "Night and Day" (Monty Woolley had advised him to give it up) and decided to spend the weekend at "Beechwood," Vincent Astor's Newport cottage. On Sunday, he joined his hostess, Helen Huntington Astor, and another guest, socialite Schuyler Livingston Parsons, for luncheon on the porch.

SCHUYLER LIVINGSTON PARSONS: A summer rainstorm was in progress and as we dined, Mrs. Astor became unnerved by the noise caused by a broken drainpipe and said, "I must have that eave mended at once. That drip, drip, drip is driving me mad."
    Cole jumped up from the table, saying "I think that will work!" He immediately went to the piano, where for the first time, the complete version of "Night and Day" was played. Helen Astor's comment became "the drip, drip, drip of the raindrops," which no previous amount of hard work had turned up.

COLE PORTER: Adele Astaire had just married Lord Charles Cavendish, son of the Duke and Duchess of Devonshire (another son would wed Kathleen Kennedy, sister of the future president), and I wanted to star Fred Astaire alone. Such a thing as one Astaire had never been heard of on Broadway. I thought that it would be an excellent idea, though Fred was more than a trifle dubious about the whole business.

In a letter to George Byron, dated June 30, 1953, Cole told the following anecdote about the song "After You, Who?":

> I shall always be grateful to "After You" because I had been engaged by Dwight Wiman for *Gay Divorce*. Our great hope was to persuade Fred Astaire to play the lead.
>
> We were living in Paris at the time and I asked Fred to the house to hear what I had written so far. Once I played "After You," he decided to do the show.

The musical *Gay Divorce*, with book by Dwight Taylor, later became the movie *Gay Divorcée*. The play opened in Boston to very bad notices. Fred Astaire was as touchy as gunpowder at the opening. He reportedly complained bitterly to the producers, Dwight Wiman and Tom Weatherly, that his voice would be ruined if he tried to sing "Night and Day." Weatherly called in Cole and ordered him to drop the song from the score, but Cole, after numerous conversations with Fred, convinced him to keep trying to work with the number.

"Night and Day" was unique among Porter songs. There were forty-eight bars instead of the thirty-two bars traditional in songs up to that time. And because Fred Astaire's voice had a small range that sounded best on certain notes, it was in this show that Porter began his practice of composing a song to make use of a singer's natural assets and bypass any weaknesses.

Gay Divorce opened at New York's Ethel Barrymore Theatre on November 29, 1932, to the total animosity of the press, who were offended by Cole's brandied friends who attended opening night in tails and decollete. It finally came through, running 248 performances, after a dosage of cut-rate tickets, but it was a close call for quite a while.

Linda Porter continued the tradition she established with *The New Yorkers* opening, this time presenting Cole with a two-tone gold cigarette case of yellow and pink gold in a stripe pattern that formed stars, and had a catch set with sapphires. The end panel of the Cartier case was engraved *"Gay Divorce, November 7, 1932,"* the date the play had opened in New Haven.

A London production, also starring Fred Astaire and Claire Luce, opened at the Palace Theatre November 2, 1933, running for 180 performances.

Besides "Night and Day," other Porter tunes in the musical included Fred Astaire's favorite from the show, "After You, Who?" and "I've Got You on My Mind." "Night and Day" caught on after about three months, then flared all over the world into Cole's biggest hit yet.

COLE PORTER: My wife and I left for Europe after the show opened and we were very disappointed that no one seemed to like the song; Fred was the only one who recorded the song at the outset.

IRVING BERLIN (TO PORTER): I am mad about "Night and Day" and think it is your high spot. You probably know it is being played all over and all the orchestra leaders think it is the best tune of the year, and I agree with them.

Brooks Atkinson/*The New York Times:* Mr. Porter's tunes and lyrics have the proper dash and breeding. . . . One might be more fervent about Mr. Porter's score if he had good voices to sing it. But Mr. Astaire and Miss Claire Luce, being singers only by necessity, make the chief song numbers of *Gay Divorce* perfunctory.

The New Yorker: There are songs by Mr. Cole Porter, dances by Fred Astaire and Claire Luce, and, in short, everything to raise one's spirits in anticipation.... And Mr. Porter, if not quite up to his usual stuff, is still impish enough in music and lyrics. . . .

WALTER WINCHELL: This intimate musical is blessed with Cole Porter songs, all of them being fascinating rhythms and tunes.

New York News: Cole Porter, runner-up to George Gershwin as a composer of stunning rhythms, has done the music and lyrics, and both are a cut above the usual. . . .

DESPITE REPEATED REQUESTS that he return to New York, Cole decided to remain in Europe and work on an offer from Charles Cochran for a musical version of James Laver's novel, *Nymph Errant.* The plan was to persuade Gertrude Lawrence to play the heroine and to entrust the libretto to Romney Brent, a Spanish-American who was at the time appearing in the London production of Noel Coward's *Words and Music,* and who was far better known as an actor than a playwright.

COLE CONTINUED TO shock European society with his innovative ways when he introduced a Chicago-born cabaret singer, Bricktop, to Parisian society and then insisted that the light-skinned, red-haired black woman be invited to the opening of the Paris opera season. He enlisted the aid of his friend (and wife's couturier) Captain Edward Molyneux, who at first demurred at the idea of creating a dress for a Negro, especially since Cole had selected exactly the same dress that the Irish-born Molyneux was designing for Princess Marina of Greece (later to become the Duchess of Kent).

Cole reminded his friend that Linda Porter spent far more in one season in his salon than the entire Greek royal family. That remark was enough to ensure that Bricktop would be gowned by one of the leading designers in France and would sweep into the opera on the arm of her friend Cole Porter. French society was indignant, and the Paris press went wild in reporting the anger.

BRICKTOP: A lot of people thought that Cole Porter was a strange man—cold, indifferent, rude. But I didn't know that Cole Porter. He was shy, that's true, and shy people have problems, especially if they have any celebrity at all. He wasn't very good at dealing with hurly-burly newspapermen or with other people who might not be as well-mannered as he was. If you were going to be pushy with Cole, you had to do it with flair, like Elsa Maxwell did. He couldn't stand plain snobs or social climbers, and as I've said, he'd go out of his way not to be rude, even to total strangers. He could have told off a lot of singers, but he preferred to leave by the back way rather than offend them.

COLE PORTER: I'm not a snob. I just want the best of everything.

ROMNEY BRENT: After all, he was Cole Porter. He had written four or five big productions. But he was easy to work with, this man. What there was about him was an overwhelming sense of style and drama. . . .

Nymph Errant opened at London's Adelphi Theatre on October 6, 1933, running 154 performances. In addition to Gertrude Lawrence, the cast included Iris Ashley, Moya Nugent, Queenie Leonard, and Elisabeth Welch. An all-girl sextet was part of the show and one of its members was Sheila Marlyn, later to gain fame as Hollywood columnist Sheilah Graham.

None of Porter's tunes from *Nymph Errant* gained lasting success. Among them was the beautiful "Experiment" (a great favorite of the late Mabel Mercer), "It's Bad for Me," and "Solomon." Even with a good score, a great cast and the brilliant choreography of Agnes de Mille, the show faded from memory, never making it to New York.

Despite the mixed reaction to *Nymph Errant,* Cole Porter once told his friend Dr. Albert Sirmay, who was also an editor for the music publisher Chappell and Co., that the libretto was the best he'd ever had and that the score was the best he'd ever done. Fox Pictures paid $25,000 for film rights, and planned to star Alice Faye in the movie version. The same studio later wanted to bring it to the screen with Julie Andrews, and Miss Andrews did sing "The Physician" from *Nymph Errant* in *Star,* the film biography of Gertrude Lawrence.

The only American production of *Nymph Errant* was a well received one mounted by the Equity Library Theatre, March 11-April 4, 1982. This production left the book for the most part as it was in the original production; there was one rewrite of about two pages to alter the racial attitude toward a character.

If *Nymph Errant* failed to catch on in its debut, the opening night was a huge success for its composer. Lady Emerald Cunard gave another of her lavish supper parties for Cole Porter. Newsmen and photographers camped on her doorstep to take note of all the fashionable people entering to pay homage to the brash young American songwriter. Even the Prince of Wales arrived, with Lady Furness on one arm and Wallis Simpson on the other.

Cole liked fashionable people and elaborate parties, partly because they genuinely amused him (just as poor people and makeshift celebrations depressed him), and partly because ideas for songs flowed swiftly through his mind in the midst of these bejeweled throngs.

In contrast to those writers who isolated themselves and would sweat in lonely turmoil over their work, Cole relaxed at a party. He would drink champagne and arrive home at dawn with a fairly complete outline of a new song, sometimes based on something that had been said. "You're the Top," for example, had its origin one night during supper at the Boeuf sur le Toit in Paris, when Cole and Mrs. Alastair Mackintosh entertained themselves by making up a list of superlatives that rhymed.

Another Porter song, "Miss Otis Regrets," was the result of an evening at Yale classmate Len Hanna's New York apartment when one of the guests turned on the radio and picked up a cowboy lament. It sounded so terrible to Cole that he sat down at the piano and began to burlesque it in tortured whines that gradually formed a new song. As the music and lyrics took shape, Monty Woolley, who had wagered Cole that he could not write a song that fit the title he had suggested, hastily borrowed a morning coat from Hanna's butler and silver tray from a maid, and reappeared as a butler, singing the first words Cole had just devised about poor Miss Otis having to cancel her lunch. His rendition launched Woolley on a career as a wit and brought to the surface his great talent as a mimic that eventually led to his starring role in *The Man Who Came to Dinner.*

Cole immediately dedicated the song to Elsa Maxwell. Bricktop, who always included the number in her nightclub act, laid claim to the song, and announced to her audiences that Cole had written it for her. This was not so. Although the song never attained popularity in America—it was just too offbeat and sophisticated for the average American's taste—it was a big hit in England and, oddly enough, sold over 100,000 copies of sheet music in Hungary and the Scandinavian countries.

MONTY WOOLLEY: Cole and I were sitting in the bar of the 21 Club one afternoon, when in walked Peggy Hopkins Joyce [a sometimes showgirl who enjoyed parties and the social whirl, but was also known as the world's greatest collector of diamonds, all given to her by her male admirers]. In the course of our conversation with Miss Joyce, who had just arrived from

Europe, she confided to us that she had to flee Monte Carlo because it was full of such dreadful people. She said that a companion tried to reassure her that despite this invasion, there were still a great many attractive people. Peggy recalled asking her friend, "For ninstance, whom?"

Cole loved the story and years later this phrase turned up in the verse of "It Ain't Etiquette," sung by Bert Lahr in *Du Barry Was a Lady*; the phrase became "Now, for ninstance."

NO COMPOSER BEFORE or since balanced a life lived in the glitzy world of show business and the glamorous world of high society as well as Cole Porter. As Cole and Linda continued to skim along, living a seven-parties-a-night life on two continents, the peripatetic composer also combined the fun of these worlds with the very strenuous life of a working songwriter. These two sides of Cole Porter's life may have seemed incongruous, but the heavy social life appeared to feed his creativity and made Cole Porter *the* American composer of the thirties.

Soon the worlds of show business and high society would combine to create a glittering new social phenomenon to be dubbed Café Society.

"You're the Top"

IF NOT A snob, Cole Porter and his music had great snob appeal. And the composer was indeed at the top! Both he and Linda were in the forefront of a new social order that had begun to take form during the late 1920s and was firmly established by the thirties—Café Society.

They were founding members of this often-screwball social set and served on its imaginary governing council. The titular head of this nomadic tribe was the boyish, effete Prince of Wales, who in later incarnations became the reluctant King Edward VIII and later the estranged Duke of Windsor. The daily chores of publicizing this elite corps fell to press agents, columnists, and photographers, and foremost among this group were two corpulent homosexuals and a squat, unattractive lesbian: Lucius Beebe, a Boston Brahman who coined the phrase "Café Society" and served as its Merlin; Maury Paul, "Cholly Knickerbocker" to the Hearst press, was its court jester; and Elsa Maxwell doubled as a publicist and flamboyant hostess.

Vogue (**February 1938**): Within the past year or two there appeared in New York a new, colorful, prodigal social army, the ranks of which are made up of rich, carefree, and quite often, idle people. It is everywhere known as Café Society.

Apparently, the votaries of the new cult prefer to go to bed at dawn; to dance—with the endurance of dervishes—at night clubs; to dine well and drink late in cafes. They have been heralded as restless and haunted spirits who, three times a day, wave at one another in an ecstasy of amazed recognition, first at the Colony, then at "21," and finally, after midnight, at El Morocco. . . .

BRICKTOP: Linda Porter was a great lady. When Cole first began to take an interest in me, she made no objection to his efforts. As a Southern-born woman, she naturally was curious about blacks who had made their mark in the world, and once she asked me a question that was probably only important to one of her background: would I rather be white than Negro? I answered readily, "I don't want to offend you, Mrs. Porter, but to be white and poor? Never!" She seemed satisfied with my answer.

SCOTT FITZGERALD: My greatest claim to fame is that I discovered Bricktop before Cole Porter.

ARNOLD WHITRIDGE: I was introduced to my wife by Cole Porter. In the early years of our marriage, we saw Cole and Linda often, dining with them in Paris and New York. These were joyous years and I remember well that many evenings would end with Cole sitting down at the piano and both of us would sing the songs from his earliest years, especially those he composed during our undergraduate days at Yale.

ELSA MAXWELL: Among other delights, Cole is fun!

LUCIUS BEEBE: The personnel of one of Miss Maxwell's parties resembled the ultimate tops in New York celebrities. At one table there was Cole Porter, Tallulah Bankhead, William Gaxton, Mrs. William Randolph Hearst, the Tommy Suffern Tailors and Harold Ross, editor of *The New Yorker*. On the dance floor, Julien Chaqueneau had for a partner Lady Peel (Beatrice Lillie) while Ethel Merman was on the arm of Prince Serge Obolensky. At another table, Mrs. T. Markoe Robertson and Miss Gladys Swarthout were vis-a-vis with Alfred de Liagre, a handsome and dashing young producer.

IT WAS WITH *Anything Goes* that Cole Porter really began to hit his stride as a composer of smash tunes. The score included such great numbers as: "Blow, Gabriel, Blow," "All Through the Night," "I Get a Kick Out of You," "You're the Top," and the title tune "Anything Goes."

COLE PORTER: *Anything Goes* was the first of my two "perfect" shows—musicals that had no tinkering whatever on them after opening night. The other, *Kiss Me, Kate,* was a tribute to assembled stagecraft of those associated with me.

ETHEL MERMAN: Before I signed my contract to appear in *Anything Goes,* I made Cole Porter play and sing the score for my parents. They vetoed two of the numbers. Cole and I liked each other immediately. He said lots of nice things about me, such as "she sounds like a band going by." People tell me he referred to me as La Merman and the Great Ethel. But the nicest thing he said was that he'd rather have me sing his songs than anybody else in the world.

I later announced that I would return the compliment. The truth is I honestly don't have either a favorite song or songwriter. When George and Ira Gershwin, Cole Porter, Irving

Berlin, Jule Styne, Steve Sondheim, and Jerry Herman have written especially for you, how are you going to pick a favorite?

COLE PORTER: I had given an audition for her mother, father, and agent. I wrote "Blow, Gabriel, Blow" for her voice. She was right on that, but I was right in sticking to my version of the others she was worried about: "You're the Top," "All Through the Night," "I Get a Kick Out of You," and "Anything Goes." This show gave me five hit standards, the peak of my career.... The next ten years were those of my greatest productivity, hampered only by my accident which finally proved to be a spur rather than a hindrance. I was to become a close friend of Ethel Merman. I never ceased to be astonished at her habit of taking down lyrics in shorthand and using her extraordinary voice in such a prodigal way. . . . Whenever Ethel opens her mouth to sing it constitutes an event for me. It was she who accounted for the fact that *Anything Goes* was the first of my two "perfect" shows.

Ethel Merman was unique, the only star ever to appear in a Cole Porter musical to have her numbers rewritten for her ("Blow, Gabriel, Blow"). This was done because he considered her a great artist and a very special friend deserving of special treatment.

Linda again presented her famous husband with another cigarette case from Cartier. The reed design had a magnificent gold and black enamel exterior. The catch was set with five cabochen-cut sapphires, and the lid was engraved *"Anything Goes,* November 5, 1934," the date the play opened in Boston.

Anything Goes opened at the Alvin Theatre in New York on November 21, 1934. In addition to Merman, the cast included William Gaxton, Bettina Hall, Victor Moore, and Vivian Vance. The book was created by P. G. Wodehouse and Guy Bolton and revised by Howard Lindsay and Russel Crouse. Howard Lindsay also staged the show.

The production had everything that would endear it to both critics and public alike: an excellent score, good book, top-notch direction and brilliant casting. Ethel Merman played an evangelist-turned-nightclub-singer; Victor Moore, the sad-voiced comic, played Public Enemy Number 13 who in the show comes aboard a boat disguised as a clergyman; and singer Billy Gaxton stowed aboard to be near his society sweetheart, played by Bettina Hall.

The uproarious show added up to a great evening in the theater and ran for a record 420 performances. The provocative "You're the Top" was an instant success and was heard for the better part of a year all over America.

The New York Times: By keeping their sense of humor uppermost, they have made a thundering good musical show out of *Anything Goes,* which was put on at the Alvin last evening. They are Guy Bolton and P. G. Wodehouse, whose humor is completely unhackneyed; Cole Porter has written a dashing score with impish lyrics. . . . "You're the Top" is one of the most congenial songs Mr. Porter has written.

The New Yorker: Any show which has Cole Porter writing its music and lyrics needs hardly to try out in the provinces. Mr. Porter is in a class by himself as a writer of original lyrics, and unless I do not know my theatregoers, the town will shortly be driving itself crazy trying to memorize the series of things indicating the "Top." In this one song, he has summarized American civilization better than any symposium of national thinkers has ever been able to do.

Anything Goes was Ethel Merman's first big starring role on Broadway. Cole's response to her had been love at first sight— or rather, first sound.

<u>ETHEL MERMAN:</u>   What Cole had done was to analyze my voice and turn out songs which showed off its variety. "You're the Top" brought people to their feet because it was a new kind of love song . . . there had never been a song like it before, a complete original. So I wasn't surprised that at the peak of its popularity, Cole received 300 parodies a month.

<u>WALTER KERR:</u>   I always think of her standing still and belting. I don't know why. I'm sure she did stand still once while she was first singing "Let's Be Buddies" in whatever triumphant show that was.

Ethel Merman continued to make Broadway history in future Cole Porter productions—a total of five, something of a landmark in show business.

BEFORE THE OPENING of *Anything Goes,* the film version of *Gay Divorce* (retitled *Gay Divorcée*) was released late in 1934 and starred Fred Astaire and Ginger Rogers together for the first time. "Night and Day" was the only song from the Porter score used in the movie.

If Fred Astaire made a great dancer out of Ginger Rogers, it is equally true that Ginger made a successful romantic lead out of Astaire. He had been handicapped in his early Broadway career by the simple fact that Adele, who had been his dancing partner, was his sister, thereby requiring librettists to devise tortuous plot complications in order to introduce a love interest without any suggestion of incest. But now he was free to court Ginger Rogers, as well as dance with her, in the movies with perfect propriety. Ginger had an alert, friendly, distinctively American charm that perfectly complemented his jaunty screen personality. In real life, both were equally assiduous and competitive, and both had the determination to become recognized screen presences.

Within a year of this collaboration, Astaire and Rogers had become the greatest money-making team in Hollywood history. They went on to give the public seven more pictures, including *Top Hat, Follow the Fleet, Shall We Dance,* and *Carefree.*

"Night and Day," used in the first Astaire-Rogers film, remains a standard to this day and provides a five-figure income to Cole's heirs. ASCAP rates "Night and Day" among its top money-earners of all time. Ironically, the first Academy Award for a song used in a film was awarded to a non-Porter tune from *Gay Divorcée*—"The Continental."

NOT YET A Hollywood name, Cole continued to work on Broadway, making every effort to top, or at least match, the success he had enjoyed with *Anything Goes.* What he really needed to achieve this goal was a collaborator whose wit and charm matched his own.

MOSS HART: I thought to myself one evening with them [Linda and Cole] what fun it would be to do a musical with Cole Porter. I dismissed this conceit quickly, yet later, that is exactly what happened. We did do a musical together; moreover, we sailed around the world to write it, and I learned to my chagrin that the jaunty and debonair world of Cole Porter disappeared completely when he was at work, and that Linda was a stern and jealous guardian of that work.

The enterprise that was ultimately to emerge in 1935 was the musical *Jubilee.* In spite of the Depression and the New Deal, everyone was singing his songs: "You're the Top," "I Get a Kick Out of You," and "Blow, Gabriel, Blow" from *Anything Goes,* which had opened three nights before.

"I think I came to a decision this morning," I said, "I'm going to drop work completely for a while. There are always ideas, there are always plays to be written—but always at the expense of something else. I don't want to settle for that quick trip to Europe wedged in between work and rehearsals—I want to see the whole damned world and I want to see it now. I'm going to take a year off and racket around the world."

Cole looked at me soberly. "Why not do both?" he said. "I like that idea of yours for a musical. Why don't we do it and go around the world at the same time?"

I looked at him with the same wonder that had made me laugh when I had watched him put on the new gold garter in Paris: "Why not?" he persisted. "I could leave next week, couldn't you?" He was already making his way toward the door. "Let's stop by Cook's and find the first round-the-world sailing, and then go back to the hotel and tell Linda."

This was Wednesday. The next ship around the world was to sail the following Tuesday. We were on it.

Cole and Linda went aboard the Cunard White Star Liner *Franconia* with twenty-seven pieces of luggage. In addition to this, Cole brought along a small piano-organ, metronome, typewriter, pencils, an ample supply of music paper, a phonograph, and six cases of Perrier-Jouët champagne.

While the pre-midnight festivities were going on prior to sailing, Cole's collaborators from *Anything Goes*, Howard Lindsay and Russel Crouse, sent aboard a large crate to be delivered to Cole's stateroom. On opening it, Cole found a large, ugly statue of a woman with a bulging figure. It was expected that as soon as the ship left port, Cole would toss it overboard. But given Cole's great sense of the ridiculous, he ordered the grotesque statue dressed in native garb for each port-of-call, and he staged elaborate cocktail parties in her honor.

COLE PORTER: I wrote the song ["Begin the Beguine"] aboard the *Franconia* after witnessing a native dance at Kalabahi, a small village on the Island of Alor [one of the Sunda Islands in the former Dutch Indies].

<u>MOSS HART:</u>   It did not surprise me too greatly when later on, after we had left Samoa, he informed me that one of the chief ballads for the show was to be "Begin the Beguine." The Beguine was a native dance we had driven endless hot miles to witness. I had reservations about the length of the song. Indeed, I am somewhat ashamed to record that I thought it had ended when he was only halfway through playing it. But I was much relieved that our chief love song was not to be about koala bears or a duckbilled platypus which he had found entertaining.

In a letter dated March 23, 1945, to Frank Colby of Houston, Texas, who had inquired about the song, Cole's reply gives another version of how the song developed:

> I was living in Paris at the time and somebody suggested that I go see Black Martinquois, many of whom live in Paris, do their native dance, the Beguine, in a remote nightclub on the Left Bank of the Seine. This I did quickly, and I was very much taken by the rhythm of the dance. The rhythm was practically that of the already-popular rumba but much faster. The moment I saw it, I thought of "Begin the Beguine" as a good title for a song and put it away in a notebook, adding a memorandum as to its rhythm and tempo. About ten years later while going around the world we stopped at an island in the Lesser Sunda Islands, to the west of New Guinea, at a place called "Kalabahi." My spelling of Kalabahi is entirely phonetic. A native dance was started for us, of which the melody of the first four bars would become my song. . . .

The cruise around the world produced another song that would also become a hit. It was introduced by Ethel Merman and Bob Hope in Cole Porter's 1936 production *Red, Hot and Blue,* and Bob Hope still uses "It's De-Lovely" in his numerous worldwide appearances. Again, as with most Cole Porter tunes, we have a number of versions as to its origin.

COLE PORTER: I took a world tour a couple of years ago, and I was in Java with Monty Woolley and Moss Hart. We'd just been served that famous eastern fruit—the mangosteen—and we were all enjoying it mightily. . . . Moss Hart said, "It's delightful!" I chimed in with, "It's delicious!" and Monty Woolley said, "It's de-lovely!" and there's the title of the song.

COLE PORTER (ANOTHER VERSION):   In 1935, when my wife and I and Monty Woolley were approaching the harbor of Rio de Janeiro by boat, I had risen especially for the event, but Mr. Woolley had stayed up all night to see it, and during the night he had enjoyed a few whiskies and sodas. As we stood in the bow of the boat my exclamation was, "It's delightful!" My wife followed with, "It's delicious!" And Monty in his happy state cried, "It's de-lovely!" This last exclamation gave me the title for the song.

At the time of the trip, thirty-year-old Moss Hart already had two big stage hits to his credit, *Merrily We Roll Along* and *As Thousands Cheer*, both written in collaboration with George S. Kaufman. Moss was a shy, slender, black-haired man with an urbane manner that immediately appealed to Cole.

During their first meeting in the bar of the Hotel Ritz in Paris, Hart was witness to one of Cole's frequent extravagant gestures. The young writer had been asked by a friend of Cole's to deliver a pair of eighteen-karat gold garter clasps. Cole fastened the new garter clasps in place and tossed the old gold ones across the bar to the barman.

By the time the *Franconia* docked in New York on May 31, 1935, Hart had completely finished the book and Cole had virtually all the songs assembled for *Jubilee*. Among them were

"Begin the Beguine," "A Picture of Me Without You," "Why Shouldn't I?" and "The Kling-Kling Bird on the Divi-Divi Tree." Another tune for the show, "Just One of Those Things," was written during a trip that fall with Hart to Len Hanna's estate in Ohio.

Jubilee was a big, beautiful spectacle, and the Boston audience loved it. It seemed to be just what America needed for entertainment during the height of the Depression.

The show opened in New York at the Imperial Theatre on October 12, 1935. Veteran actress Mary Boland, Melville Cooper, and June Knight headed the cast. Among the supporting cast were Charles Walters, Ted Fetter, Mark Plant, and Montgomery Clift.

EARL BLACKWELL: I came to New York from California on a brief visit in 1935. I arrived the night that *Jubilee* opened at the Imperial Theatre. I was lucky enough to get standing room. As the curtain went up I spotted Joan Crawford and Franchot Tone coming into the theatre. They had just been married.

There was this friend of mine from Hollywood that I thought I recognized and when I heard him sing, I knew it was he— Charles Walters, who later went on to become a well-established Hollywood director, directing Judy Garland in *Easter Parade* and Ginger Rogers and Fred Astaire in *The Berkeley's of Broadway*. He had a featured role in the play as the Young Prince James. Montgomery Clift was also in the cast. So I went backstage after the show and met Cole Porter for the first time. Although I never got to know him well, he was one of the few celebrities that I admired tremendously. I got to know him socially a little better after his accident in 1937.

What brought me to New York from Hollywood in 1937 was that I had written this play, *April Fool,* and Peggy Fears, a former Ziegfeld Follies star and the wife of A. C. Blumenthal, took an option on it for $75 a month for the entire year. She said she wanted Jerome Kern to write the music; then thinking better of it, she said, "No, I think it's better for Cole," and I thought, "My God, Cole Porter writing music for my book." But then Peggy didn't follow through. That was just one of my dreams in those early days.

He was one of the few people I can think of with all the money in the world and with tremendous talent, who continued to use his talent. He didn't have to compose. He contributed so much to the world of theatre, and the world of motion pictures, too.

The press called *Jubilee* the ultimate "post-Ziegfeld" show, an extravaganza of gorgeous costumes and colorful scenery.

The New Yorker: Oddly enough, the chief virtue of *Jubilee*, which sets out so doggedly to be sophisticated, is its simple naivete. The lyrics, which Mr. Cole Porter has devised with an eye to pleasing perhaps eighteen people, are negligible in market value. His music is, I have a feeling, better than he knows, because he has hidden his most valuable tunes in incidental choruses, such as the entrance of the ladies-in-waiting at the beginning of the last act (really something). . . .

The main point is that Messrs. Moss Hart, Cole Porter, Hassard Short, Max Gordon (everybody's sweetheart) and Sam Harris have a show in *Jubilee* which is heartwarming and beautiful, and I hope it runs forever, because it is so nice.

Newsweek: Moss Hart and Cole Porter placated America last week. . . . It was rumored on Broadway that Cole Porter had decided, with *Jubilee,* to write music that, for a change, would not overshadow its surroundings, but in attempting to live up to this resolution, he chose the wrong time to be strong-willed, for *Jubilee* had the need for his slickest, most inventive compositions.

Linda commissioned Cartier to design another commemorative gold cigarette case for Cole. This one was done in eighteen-karat pink and yellow gold, again with a reeded motif and inside lid engraved with the show's title and opening date.

In addition to Linda's gift, Cole was also the recipient of a presentation case from his best friend, Howard Sturges. It, too, was designed by Cartier but fashioned in silver and red leather, with "*Jubilee,* 1935" engraved outside. Inside it read, "Cole, from Uncle Howard."

A SERIES OF bad luck incidents backstage defeated *Jubilee.* On several occasions, fires broke out backstage. From time to time the show's star, Mary Boland, took too many nips from the bottle before going on, often resulting in an erratic performance. Finally her agent secured her release from the show so she could return to Hollywood for a multi-picture deal. The producers brought in as her replacement Laura Hope Crews, a fine actress, but without the same name power or comic assets of Mary Boland there were fewer paying customers. Without its star, *Jubilee* folded after only 169 performances.

The usually unflappable Cole was so angry with Miss Boland that he vowed she would never work in another show of his. Another vow he took was to never invest in a show involving his songs—his $15,000 investment (which was a considerable amount of money in the thirties) in *Jubilee* went down the drain.

Cole Porter and Moss Hart never collaborated again after *Jubilee.* Occasionally they would discuss the possibility of doing another show, but nothing ever came of it. Hart went on to greater theatrical glory as a playwright with George S. Kaufman, and into a happy marriage with actress Kitty Carlisle in 1946. He and Cole remained good friends and over the years would run into one another at Broadway openings or at one of Manhattan's social gatherings.

Just prior to the closing of *Jubilee,* Cole did the predictable. He and Linda, along with Moss Hart and Newport social lioness Mrs. Herman Oelrichs, sailed for Bermuda, where for three weeks they occupied the beachfront estate of real-estate mogul Vincent Astor, as Cole assuaged his disappointment over his recent Broadway effort. Not only did he have to recover from the show's closing, but also from the fact that none of the songs from *Jubilee* became an overnight success.

On their return from Bermuda, Cole and Linda followed Elsa Maxwell by moving into the Waldorf Towers, the private apartment building alongside the Waldorf-Astoria on Manhattan's Park Avenue. The Porters leased a huge apartment for the very nominal fee of $35 a day, because the management, under the guidance of Miss Maxwell, hoped their presence would help popularize the building. Later, when Linda's health had deteriorated to the point where Cole's late-night piano playing disturbed her, the Porters traded the large apartment for two somewhat smaller ones located directly opposite one another on the forty-first floor.

COLE PORTER: "Begin the Beguine," which I wrote for *Jubilee*, died in the show in 1935. The only critic who mentioned it was Robert Benchley, who said, "Why throw in just another rumba?" In 1940 Artie Shaw made a swing version of it—and I've been eating off it ever since. Years later, Benchley used to hang out in a club on the Sunset Strip. Whenever I would walk in, the band would play "Begin the Beguine." Bob would hide his face behind a napkin and say, "I know, I know."

ARTIE SHAW: "Begin the Beguine" paid my rent.

HAZEL MEYER: Take "Begin the Beguine" for instance. It's a likely choice because, as a show tune automatically published as sheet music in 1935 by reason of its inclusion in *Jubilee*, it was a dismal flop from Tin Pan Alley's viewpoint. It sold few copies and remained singularly unnoticed until bandleader Artie Shaw* recorded it for Victor Bluebird Records in 1938. "Begin the Beguine" was a popular hit song, a delayed hit, and is one of the most valuable properties in popular music. It's an indestructible standard.

FINALLY IT WAS time to go to Hollywood, and with this move, the Porters' life-style took on a new dimension. Cole and Hollywood had flirted with each other during the early thirties. There were plans to use his work in *Star Dust* and *Adios Argentina*, but neither one was produced, and some of Cole's best-known songs were salvaged from the wreckage of these projects. "I Get a Kick Out of You" had been taken from *Star Dust* to become one of his biggest hits in *Anything Goes*, and "Don't Fence Me In," a casualty of *Adios Argentina*, would languish for ten years before being sung by Roy Rogers in *Hollywood Canteen*. In wartime America, the song extolled all that was pure and good in rural American life and the homey song became one of Cole's top moneymakers.

The 1934 release of *Gay Divorcée* was the real beginning of Cole Porter's long association with the film industry and California. Cole always enjoyed a new challenge and Hollywood was indeed just that—a totally new business for him and a very different cast of characters.

MGM summoned him to Hollywood to write songs for an Eleanor Powell/James Stewart film titled *Born to Dance*. His initial contract called for $75,000 for the twenty weeks it took to make the film—an offer he could hardly refuse. The Porters rented as their first Hollywood home the luxurious estate of silent film actor Richard Barthelmess. It was the kind of house that befitted one of the great old stars, with well-manicured lawns, tennis courts, and a big swimming pool.

---

*Xavier Cugat recorded the tune first for Victor in an outstanding arrangement that nevertheless failed to catch on.

Unfortunately, Linda, despite the plush quarters, disliked both California and the film colony from the very outset and made her feelings known to both Cole and her East Coast friends. The climate had a deleterious effect on her already fragile respiratory system, and the film crowd did not fascinate her the way legitimate stage stars and the Café Society crowd had.

She also loathed the Hollywood custom of combining business and social affairs and totally disapproved of the hard drinking that prevailed, holding with the civilized conviction that strong drink destroyed one's ability to enjoy fine cuisine. A very light drinker herself, she bristled at dining with guests in various stages of intoxication. In time, she set a two-cocktail limit before dinner. Cole, who actually preferred three or four drinks, deferred to her wishes, a custom he continued even when Linda was not present.

While Cole shared Linda's contempt for the ex-glove salesmen and onetime furriers who had become movie moguls, he "went Hollywood quickly and completely," in the words of gossip columnist Dorothy Kilgallen. "I like it here," he told her, "It's like living on the moon, isn't it? When I first came here they told me, 'You'll be so bored, you'll die; nobody talks about anything but pictures.' After I was here a week, I discovered that I didn't want to talk about anything else myself."

Despite her reservations, Linda realized that her husband reveled in the atmosphere, and for a time she toyed with the idea of buying or building a house in California. Since Linda's health made long-range plans in Hollywood impossible, the Porters made do by renting lavish homes in the film capital. After the Barthelmess house, they leased the home of Richard Cromwell on their second trip and then finally a lovely home at 416 North Rockingham in Brentwood, which was owned by actor-turned-interior-decorator William Haines. This luxurious residence would be the Porters' base of operations on the West Coast for the rest of their lives.

In mid-June of 1936 Cole returned to New York, looking forward to the release of MGM's *Born to Dance* and Paramount's first version of *Anything Goes** with Ethel Merman in the role she created on Broadway. Unfortunately, Paramount's choice of Bing Crosby resulted in a musical not at all to Cole's liking. He took it in stride, however, and was consoled by the fact that Paramount provided half the backing for his next Broadway production, which would have again his favorite star—La Merman.

Born to Dance was the only film in which James Stewart sang. He did a creditable job on Porter's "Easy to Love." Another song from the film that became a standard, "I've Got You Under My Skin," was introduced in the film by Virginia Bruce.

THE REHEARSAL OF *Red, Hot and Blue* began a monumental struggle between the agents of Ethel Merman and Jimmy Durante. The contracts had not spelled out which star was to have top billing on the preferred left-hand side. For a time it seemed the show might lose one of its stars, for neither star would accede to the other's demand. Then Cole stepped in and suggested a compromise that allowed Jimmy Durante and Ethel Merman to share the billing by having their names criss-cross above the show's title. By alternating the location of the names every week, neither would have the advantage over the other.

While this diplomatic suggestion saved the cast for his show, Cole's working style exhibited traits that sometimes baffled those working with him. He could be by turns pensive, agitated, and polite. When interested or amused, he talked with a great rush of words that betrayed a slight lisp; bored, he withdrew within a room as completely as if he had walked away.

---

*There were two film versions. This first of the two Paramount versions of the 1934 stage musical starred Bing Crosby, Ethel Merman, and Ida Lupino. A 1955 version also starred Bing Crosby and had a new book, but retained the original Cole Porter score. This version was directed by stage great Bobby Lewis.

Occasionally during a silent period, he would contribute a private thought on whatever he happened to be writing.

At one rehearsal of the musical, Cole walked past Russel Crouse, one of the co-authors, about twelve times without speaking. Crouse wondered what he had done to offend Cole and was about to ask him when, at six o'clock in the evening, Cole came up to him, laid a friendly hand on his shoulder, and said firmly, "In my pet pailletted gown." It turned out that he had simply been trying all day to think of the right line for a lyric.

Red, Hot and Blue, starring Ethel Merman and Jimmy Durante and featuring Bob Hope in his Broadway debut, opened on October 29, 1936, at the Alvin Theatre.

Cole loved opening nights, especially his own. Much of his legend grew out of the reporting of these glamorous events. Audiences came early to Porter's first nights just to see the entrance of the Porters and their party. The Porters and their guests always arrived on time, sweeping in on a wave of chatter, perfume, furs, and jewels to their seats in the middle of the second row. Fascinated columnists would inform their readers just what opening-night tokens the Porters had given each other on the occasion of the out-of-town opening. On this occasion, Cole had given Linda a beautiful bracelet and matching clips embellished with 80-karat-sapphire, 36-karat-emerald, and 48-karat-ruby leaves set along a diamond branch and designed by Cartier. Linda presented Cole with a platinum cigarette case with rubies and sapphires on the top and the signs of the zodiac in green and gold on the bottom. The case was designed by the Porters' friend, the Duc di Verdura.

Unfortunately, Linda was far too ill to actually attend the opening of *Red, Hot and Blue.* Earlier, Cole was a guest at the wedding of his great friend William Rhinelander Stewart to a great society beauty, Janet Newbold Ryan. The newlyweds gave a dinner in the Iridium Room of the St. Regis in honor of

Cole Porter, Mary Pickford, Merle Oberon, and Leonard Hanna; following this party the guests went on to the opening of *Red, Hot and Blue.*

As was his habit, Cole would stroll up the aisle during intermission to chat with friends. He'd often be heard to say, in a tone of honest admiration, "Good, isn't it?"

Good it wasn't. *Red, Hot and Blue* was a disappointment for all concerned and ended its Broadway run after only 183 performances.

KATE PORTER: I don't like his new show, *Red, Hot and Blue.* It's too rowdy. It's not my style, but it is funny.

Newsweek: Cole Porter is the great disappointment. He can usually be relied upon for the most haunting tunes of the theatrical season, but this time his torch songs are second-rate.

The New York Times: Anything goes for a laugh in *Red, Hot and Blue,* which opened at the Alvin last evening. For this is the old Lindsay-Crouse-Porter-Merman combination which set the town on its ear two seasons ago.

In Miss Merman's honor, Porter has scribbled off a few good songs. Not a whole trunkful, for some of them are mediocre. But he can roll off a smart bolero now and then—"Down in the Depths of the 90th Floor," where Miss Merman eats out her heart fortissimo; "It's De-Lovely," in which Miss Merman and Bob Hope hop-scotch through some remarkable lyrics to an exultant refrain, and "Ridin' High," which finished off the first half of the program with proper gusto. As for Miss Merman, she is still the most commanding minstrel in the business, wearing her costumes like a drum major, swinging to the music and turning the audience into a congregation of pals for the evening.

The New Yorker: Miss Merman is her usual dynamic self, and I have an idea that one or two of Mr. Cole Porter's songs benefit greatly by her powers of projection, although, on a second visit to the show, I was convinced that Mr. Porter's score is much better than I thought it the first time. Certainly, "It's De-Lovely," "A Little Skipper from Heaven Above," and "Hymn to Hymen" are first-grade, and if he wanted to make "Down in the Depths of the 90th Floor" another version of "Night and Day," he had a perfect right to. His lyrics are, as usual, in a class by themselves.

Time: This first brand-new star to rise in Broadway's 1936–37 music-comedy firmament was judged by most observers to be second magnitude.

COLE PORTER: I just get burned by the critics. Every time I write songs for a show, they say, "The music is not up to Mr. Porter's usual standard."

It would be different if I wrote songs like Irving Berlin. People love Irving's songs the minute they hear them. They also love them twenty years later. But my songs have to grow on you.

One time my wife and I got so peeved that we decided to find out what my "standard" was. She keeps vast books of clippings, and we went back to my first Broadway show, which I did with a friend of mine from Harvard. The critics said, "These boys should leave New York and never come back!" I feel that my clash with the critics is due in large measure to the nature of my songs.

DESPITE THE CRITICS and the box office, the American public was singing and listening to Cole Porter's tunes. "I've Got You Under My Skin" leaped into second place on the list of songs most often played on the radio. "It's De-Lovely" took third place, and "Easy to Love" was twelfth.

The mid-thirties found Cole Porter a regular commuter

between Broadway and Hollywood. The increasing amount of time Cole spent on the West Coast helped trigger an estrangement between the Porters, although a far more basic reason for the rift was Cole's acceptance of the denizens of Movietown and his greed for all the delights it had to offer. Since Linda considered the film colony a sea of overblown egos sprinkled with far too much tinsel, Cole's decision to continue working part of each year in Hollywood forced her hand; she left California in the late spring of 1937 for her home in Paris.

Later that year, en route from Hollywood to Paris, Cole stopped in New York long enough to take part in an Elsa Maxwell extravaganza, a "Barnyard Frolic." Elsa had commandeered the Starlight Roof of the Waldorf-Astoria for a little fun-down-on-the-farm evening. It was attended by every Café Society celebrity who could beg, wrangle, or borrow an invitation to attend this dazzling costume ball.*

At the entrance of the Starlight Roof, there was a papier-mâché cow bedded down on real straw in a stall, and waiters dressed as farmhands poured the finest French champagne as guests entered this rustic world.

Lady Lya Abdy, a spectacular Russo-British beauty, wore red tights and a headdress made from a stuffed cow. Prince Serge Obolensky, in Russian peasant garb, led a fat, squealing pig on an 18-karat gold dog chain. Cleveland's Mrs. James A. Corrigan was dressed as a Russian monk, with a 20-karat emerald surrounded by diamonds and a double rope of Oriental pearls around her neck. Mrs. Ogden L. Mills wore a massive tiara above blue-denim overalls.

Leonard Hanna, Cole's old friend and a Cleveland multimillionaire, had imported a genuine Ohio hog caller and he was making strange cries heard above the swing band.

Mr. and Mrs. Douglas Fairbanks, Sr., Constance Bennett, and

*Under the sway of Elsa Maxwell, American society and its counterpart in Europe emulated the court of Louis XVI at Versailles, holding many lavish costume parties during the height of a world depression.

movie idol Gilbert Roland were in identical farm outfits, looking for all the world like a group of synthetic rustic quadruplets.

Among the others who frolicked in this bucolic setting were the Frederic Marches, Lauritz Melchior of the Metropolitan Opera, Princess Natalie Paley, bandleader Harry Payne Bingham, theater critic George Jean Nathan, Mrs. Vincent Astor, Charlie MacArthur of the famed Hollywood team of Hecht and MacArthur, Beatrice Lillie, fresh from her performance in *The Show Is On*, banker Winthrop Aldrich, railroad magnate W. Averell Harriman, and Cornelius Vanderbilt Whitney.

Cole Porter, attired in a cowboy outfit set off with rhinestone-heeled boots, entertained guests with lasso tricks, and dancer Ray Bolger whisked around the room with Edith Gray, sister of the Duchess of Marborough, who was dressed in a milkmaid's costume (more shades of Marie Antoinette) and more than $200,000 worth of diamond and emerald bracelets.

Presiding over all of this was Elsa Maxwell, short, snubnosed, and as frumpy in her French dance-hall girl attire as the late millionairess Hetty Green. She was the ranking hostess of two continents and sponsored, at other people's expense, New York parties that were the 1937 equivalent of the balls and cotillions of Mrs. Astor in the "Mrs. Astor requests . . ." era. Elsa's parties were vast and all-inclusive, if not always exclusive. Much to Miss Maxwell's pleasure, because of the reams of publicity they got, her parties had a tremendous hold on the public imagination.

ETHEL MERMAN: Cole had a reputation as a sophisticate and a hedonist. I suspect he capitalized on these traits. No other Broadway tunesmith enjoyed a similar image.

COLE'S PUBLIC PLEASURES were all well-documented in the press, but less well-known were his numerous private perversions, usually conducted in out-of-the-way haunts and in the company of a few intimate friends like Monty Woolley and Howard Sturges.

As he became more successful, Cole's daring and desires accelerated; his homosexual behavior was gossiped about by show people on both coasts.

From a conversation with Monty Woolley in the early 1950s, I was given insight into this other side of Cole Porter's nature. According to Woolley, both he and Cole took most of their sexual pleasures in Harlem. Harlem was regarded as the next-best thing to an anything-goes madcap heaven in Depression-bound America. Woolley, with that intensity he gave to the first reading of a play he was about to direct, extolled the physical virtues of the young black studs who inhabited the many houses of male prostitution that dotted the Harlem landscape during this period.

A favorite "house" for Cole and Monty was an establishment operated by Clint Moore. According to Woolley, Moore's brownstone was located near Striver's Row where Harlem's elite lived and where he kept an ample and much-in-demand stable of black male prostitutes. It was not far from the transvestite floor shows, sex circuses, and marijuana parlors along 140th Street.

Woolley continued painting a vivid picture of Clint Moore, his establishment, and what went on among the denizens of the "house" and its clients. It seems that Clint Moore was a history buff, particularly of Napoleon Bonaparte and the period of the First Empire, and he collected furniture and decorative objects from this period. Whenever Monty and Cole visited this house they first would spend a prolonged period in Moore's ornate offices, sipping the finest French champagne from Baccarat crystal flutes. Then Moore's newest male acquisitions were paraded around the office for their approval. Of prime importance to Monty and Cole were the looks, virility, and the studs' ability to perform and gratify every perversion.

LEONARD SPIGELGASS: Don't forget, homosexuality in that period [the 1930s] had two levels. One, it was held in major contempt, and the other was among Larry Hart and his kind [Cole Porter and Noel Coward] and it was the most exclusive club in New York.

That's terribly important to realize—that it was a club into which you couldn't get—I mean, no ordinary certified public accountant could get into the Cole Porter-Larry Hart-George Cukor world. That was their world. That was Somerset Maugham. That was Noel Coward. That was it if you were in that. And I remember those houses on 55th Street, with butlers and the carrying on . . . you were king of the golden river! That was it! In spite of the attitude toward homosexuality in those days. On the one hand, if you said, "They're homosexual," "Oh my, isn't that terrible!" was the reaction. On the other hand, if you said, "My God, the other night I was at dinner with Cole Porter," the immediate reaction was, "Jesus Christ, what did he have on? What did he say? Were you at the party? Were you at one of those Sunday brunches?" So you had this awful ambivalence.

AFTER ATTENDING ELSA'S "Barnyard Frolic" and having satisfied both the public and the private sides of his nature, Cole set sail for Europe and a hoped-for reunion with Linda. Arriving at Linda's house at 13 rue Monsieur, he found Linda still adamant in her attitude toward Hollywood and Cole's life there. During his two weeks in Paris, the Porters were never seen in public together. He stayed not at Linda's house but rather at their apartment at the Hotel Ritz. The Porters' ever-faithful friend, Howard Sturges, stayed with Linda and escorted her on the nightly round of parties.

By July 15, 1937, the strain of the separation had become too much for Cole and on the spur of the moment he decided to accompany Sturges and architect Edward Tauch on a walking tour of Germany, Italy, and Yugoslavia. Such strenuous outdoor activity for one as sybaritic as Cole seemed at odds with his image, but perhaps a brief experiment with simple pleasures fed the part of his soul left empty by constant partying.

Cole and his companions visited Munich, then went on to the music festival at Salzburg. Writing to friends, Cole extolled the majesty of the Dolomites. Early August found the trio sunning and swimming on the beaches at Dubrovnik. Ending their walking tour in late August, Cole, Sturges, and Tauch headed by train to Copenhagen and Hamlet country at Elsinore Castle. The balance of the trip was given to sightseeing in Oslo, Stockholm, and Helsinki.

With the memories of the glorious summer still fresh in his mind—it was to be his first and last walking tour ever—Cole returned to Paris on September 5, 1937, and immediately began planning the score for the Clifton Webb show, *You Never Know*.

Cole again holed up in the Ritz and avoided attending the same social events as Linda, causing a certain hardship on their many mutual friends. Linda refused to give any ground on her distaste for all things Hollywood and the accelerated and explosive sex life Cole had undertaken since entering the film colony.

On October 4, Cole telephoned a good-bye to his wife from the Ritz. He set sail aboard the *Estonia,* returning to work with Dr. Albert Sirmay, his musical editor, on the score of *You Never Know*. He also had to face the possibility of life without Linda.

"Down in the Depths"

ARRIVING IN NEW York mid-October 1937, Cole Porter set about working on the score of *You Never Know*, a musical to be produced by the Shuberts, with Clifton Webb, Lupe Velez, and torch singer Libby Holman in starring roles.

That first weekend back, Cole accepted an invitation to the Oyster Bay, Long Island, estate of American heiress Countess Edith di Zoppola. According to a number of other guests, Cole seemed to be in a highly agitated state (he had just received news from Paris that Linda was seriously considering divorce) and sought to organize the other houseguests in various recreational activities. He finally settled on horseback riding at the nearby Piping Rock Club in Locust Valley. (George Abbott disputes claims that it was Cole who decided on a riding outing. See his quote.)

Despite not having ridden for months and against the advice of the groom, the often obstinate Cole chose an extremely high-spirited mount. Soon after the party took to the bridle path, Cole's horse shied at the approach of an incline, reared, and fell, rolling over one of Cole's legs. As the terrified animal tried to right itself, it fell again on the opposite side, crushing

111

Cole's other leg. When the horse finally got to its feet Cole lay dazed, though conscious, too stunned to realize he had been severely injured. But Benjamin Moore, the first member of the party to reach him, saw that he was badly hurt and hurried to summon an ambulance.

The fire department ambulance carried Cole to a nearby hospital, where he went into shock and remained unconscious for two days.

The New York Times: COLE PORTER IS HURT IN FALL FROM HORSE.

Chicago Daily Tribune: Cole Porter's legs broken when horse falls on him.

Peru Tribune: Cole Porter seriously hurt. Mrs. Kate C. Porter, who resides east of the city, was advised in a long distance phone conversation this morning that her son, Cole Porter, will be disabled for some time as a result of injuries sustained Sunday afternoon at Long Island, New York.

The attending doctors were convinced that both legs would have to be amputated. Linda had a very frank transcontinental telephone conversation with Dr. Joseph Connolly, a brilliant orthopedic surgeon who was treating Cole, and insisted that the doctors delay any amputation until she returned to New York. (Oddly, Linda's first husband had also suffered a severe leg injury and was threatened with amputation. Linda returned to him and nursed him back to health before leaving for good.) Knowing how much stock Cole put on his appearance, Linda consulted with Cole's mother, and they reasoned together that Cole would die of despair if any part of his body was lost by amputation. She then brought in Dr. John Moorhead, an eminent bone specialist, who concurred with the women's view that such an operation would prove psychologically devastating to Cole. He told them frankly, however, that ordinarily he would agree with Dr. Connolly's recommendations. If the patient developed a high fever, he felt that amputation would still be necessary.

COLE PORTER: When this horse fell on me, I was too stunned to be conscious of the great pain, but until help came I worked on the lyrics for the song called "At Long Last Love."

JAMES OMAR COLE: I am one generation removed from Cole. My father, Jules Omar Cole, was Cole's first cousin. It was my father who really managed all the family's financial affairs. He also handled the business affairs of Westleigh Farms—Kate Porter's home, here in Peru, Indiana.

The riding accident in 1937 was both physically and psychologically devastating for him. I happened to be at school in the East at the time and I can say from firsthand observation that his total outlook was as low then as it was possible to be. Adversity was just bearing down on him in the prime of life.

But what I remember most about him at that period was his remarkable ability to achieve what he did after the accident. To think that he went on and gave the theater some of his greatest work.

GEORGE ABBOTT: The accident that caused his two legs to be broken was terribly sad, especially when you consider that he really did not want to go riding that day at the Piping Rock Club on Long Island. His friends practically mounted him on that horse against his will.

BROOKE ASTOR: Cole was such a charming man. He was a very dignified person. I went to see Cole quite often at the Waldorf Towers after that awful riding accident. I think more could have been done about his legs. Of course, today, with the progress that has been made in medical science, he would not have been crippled as he was.

I tried. I tried to bring him out of his depression with my visits. Twice I went alone and that was a disaster. I went with Billy [decorator Billy Baldwin] and I think it was good going with Billy, he was such a cheerful person.

A few days after the calamity, Elsa Maxwell and Clifton Webb visited Cole in the hospital. Even under heavy sedation, Cole made every effort to play the gracious host. On seeing Elsa, he whispered, "It just goes to show that fifty million Frenchmen can't be wrong—they eat horses instead of riding them."

For months following the accident, Cole spent most of his time at Doctor's Hospital in Manhattan, generally under heavy sedation to ease the continuous pain as surgeons worked feverishly to try to save his legs. He took his hospital stay and his medical treatment with his usual equanimity, accepting them with the same cheerful outlook generally displayed in his theatrical pursuits. Cole even gave names to his two injured limbs; Geraldine for the right leg, Josephine for the left. During the twenty-seven years of life left to him, pain was to be his constant companion.

Cole, at the suggestion of his doctors, began to discuss the pain in his right leg in a fanciful collection of notes, "A Few Illusions Caused by an Injured Anterior Popliteal Nerve."

COLE PORTER: I'm a toe dancer, but a toe dancer who dances only on the toes of his right foot. The music in the orchestra pit is charming and it's very pleasant hopping around and around to that gay tinkling strain. But after a while, I realize that my toes are tired, and, risking the reprimand of the ballet master, I decide to drop to the ball of my foot and give them a rest. But, lo

114

and behold, try as I may, I cannot do it, for my ballet slipper has been made in such a way that I must stay on the tips of my toes. So, long after the curtain has gone down, the music has stopped and I'm alone in the theatre, I watch the sad shadow I make as I go on and on, doomed forever to hop around on those poor tilted toes. It's a relief to wake up and be no longer a toe dancer. But it's an awful bore to have this tremendous new pressure on the sole of my foot, which forces it up with such incredible insistence that I feel, as if, at any moment, the tendons of my ankle would break. Gradually I get used to this, however, as it continues pushing and pushing, but I must say I become rather discouraged when late at night I look at my toes to find that they are as far away as they ever were from the shin bone.

The toes on my right foot are having a delightful time under the covers; they are tapping up and down on the cast and then resting from their exertions by stretching, and stretching so completely that each is separate from the other. This is such a pleasant feeling that it seems too good to be true. So I pull up the covers. It is *not* true.

My right leg stretches, slanting upwards before me, like the side of the hill, the summit of which is my toes. From the ankle down—and approaching me—any number of small, finely, sharply-toothed rakes are at work. Each one has about the same routine. For instance, the rake that has been allotted to the inside of my leg begins at the ankle, proceeding slowly toward the knee, and digs as deeply as it can into my skin, at times much deeper than at others, and consequently varying in its painfulness. It goes slowly on in this manner until it reaches a point just a little short of the knee, then retraces its tracks until it finds the spot where it was able to penetrate the most, at which point it settles down to dig to its heart's delight. The same procedure takes place over the entire leg and continues until I yell for a hypo.

The toes on my right foot are tapping against the cast again and once more stretching happily in the morning sun—that is, until I look at them and find that they aren't. A little later the rakes go to work, but for some reason they have reversed their procedure and instead of beginning at the ankle and digging toward the knee, they start just below the fracture and wind up at the toes. Those that mount the sole of the foot have great difficulty digging under the nails of the smaller toes, which are so close to the skin, but they finally succeed and the result is a most interesting new form of torture. In the late afternoon I notice that the right foot is doing its best to fit into a shoe that is much too short for it, but it persists and persists until someone inserts, inside the cast, a jagged glass shoehorn that extends from the inner heel all the way around to the little toe, but it is sadly ineffective and only adds to the confusion.

Even after a shot of Dilavdid has started to calm everything down, and the jagged glass shoehorn has changed into a rough stone shoehorn, it is obvious that the foot will never fit into that shoe. . . .

In time, Cole's pain reached more manageable proportions until he was able to take only minimal amounts of painkillers. But for most of his hospital stay he was a model patient. He had remarkable fortitude, rarely complaining no matter how severe the pain. He was what he had always been, a first-class gentleman with exceptional forbearance.

Despite having both legs in casts, Cole was able to celebrate Christmas of 1937 at the Waldorf Towers with Linda, whose thoughts of divorce now submerged to attend to the demands of the moment. Linda's Christmas present to Cole was another Cartier-designed gold and sapphire cigarette case, only this time the inscription read, "December 25 1937. Merry Christmas to Jo and Geraldine, Linda."

On January 17, 1938, Cole Porter was the guest of honor at a large party Elsa Maxwell tossed in the Perrouquet Suite at the Waldorf-Astoria. The purpose: a "Coming Out" party for Josephine and Geraldine in honor of having their casts removed. Among the five hundred guests* who gathered to cheer America's ailing composer were Conde Nast, Kate Porter, Baron Nicholas de Gunzberg, Mrs. Vincent Astor, Mr. and Mrs. Angier Biddle Duke, Mr. and Mrs. Benjamin Moore, Colonel and Mrs. Theodore Roosevelt, Mr. and Mrs. William Paley, Duke Fulco di Verdura, Mr. and Mrs. Winthrop Aldrich, and Mr. and Mrs. Charles Marshall.

Also present were Mr. and Mrs. William Rhinelander Stewart, Mr. and Mrs. Richard Barthelmess, Mr. and Mrs. T. Reed Vreeland, Mrs. William Woodward, and Prince Serge Obolensky.

Among the show business guests were Dorothy and Richard Rogers, George Abbott, Clifton Webb, Maxine Sullivan, Beatrice Lillie, Ethel Merman, Grace Moore, and Moss Hart.

As a climax to the festive evening, some of the guests appeared in an impromptu "miniature revue" honoring Cole. Afterward, he said that he was so filled with morphine he hadn't the foggiest notion of what was taking place, but admitted that he had loved all the attention.

COLE PORTER: From the moment I woke up in a local hospital, with both legs broken in compound fractures and an important nerve nearly cut in two, I spent months under sedatives. Through the years I underwent thirty-three operations under the jurisdiction of Dr. John J. Moorhead. For nearly a decade it was a moot question whether or not both legs would have to be

------

*I was unable to verify that Linda attended this party. If she did, it is possible that she escorted Cole to the party and then left; her respiratory problems were always aggravated by crowds; also, Linda was never very fond of Elsa Maxwell.

amputated below the knee. Luckily it proved that this was not needed.

That first year of intense pain, I did two complete shows. This was under the express orders of Dr. Moorhead. "Work!" he said emphatically. "Work as you've never worked before!"

I believed him. I think it saved my mind as well as my legs. I have always loved writing music and lyrics as nothing else in my life. My semi-doped brain seemed to be buzzing with tunes. To keep at my writing, I had my piano raised on wooden blocks and sat at it in my wheelchair. My habit of working out words and tune in my head before experimenting with it on the keyboard helped as well. I wrote *You Never Know* with Clifton Webb in mind. He had appeared in my first fiasco in 1916 as the star. There was a mutual bond between us that nothing could sever, a cord welded by that original failure and my present misery. The show was produced by the Shubert Brothers. It was a success in a small theatre in Philadelphia; put into the huge Winter Garden in New York, it became an immense flop.

<u>ELSA MAXWELL:</u>   I was an almost daily visitor and I imparted to Cole to never look back, just keep working.

Dr. Moorhead suggested at this point that Cole needed a vacation to speed the recovery process. Cole decided to spend a month in Cuba with a male nurse, Ray Kelly, and his valet, Paul Sylvain.

In Havana, Cole spent long hours on the beach baking his legs in the sun. Nights were spent making the rounds of Havana's famed bars and racy nightclubs, especially the Florida Bar,* the home of the original daiquiris, which Cole loved to down until the wee hours of the morning.

*The Florida Bar gained fame as the home-away-from-home to Ernest Hemingway.

Returning from Cuba, Cole directed his attention to completing work on the score of *You Never Know*. The show opened on March 3, 1938, in New Haven to a packed house. Then it lumbered on to Washington, Philadelphia, Pittsburgh, Detroit, Chicago, Des Moines, Indianapolis, Columbus, Buffalo and Hartford. Libby Holman left the show in Chicago in a tiff with her co-star Lupe Velez, known as "The Mexican Spitfire."

Arrangements had been made to have the show play a three-day run at the English Theatre in Indianapolis, to be sponsored by the Indianapolis Civic Theatre. Governor M. Clifford Townsend proclaimed May 23, 1938, the opening day, as "Cole Porter Day."

Those making the arrangements gave the distinct impression to others that Porter himself would be present. However, Cole declined, claiming that his health would not permit it. He designated his mother, Kate, to represent him, sending only a wire to be read by her:

> Seven months ago I had my legs knocked from under me by a very unkind and inconsiderate horse. Tonight, I find my wind knocked out of me by so much attention, and even if I were actually with you I should still be speechless. Luckily my mother, who like all good mothers has so often borne the brunt of her son's misdeeds, is here to face the music for me and I wish her much joy and happiness. It's probably the only sensation that can compare with my own deep gratitude to you for this signal honor.

After all the salvos had been fired in Cole's honor, another matter surfaced—the Civic Theatre committee found itself in the red and sought Cole's assistance in getting the Shuberts to forgo the hefty guarantee that they had demanded from the locals.

Sending Cole a scrapbook and a specially minted medallion

as a momento of the occasion, the committee enclosed a polite note asking that the composer intercede with the Shuberts, asking to cut in half the Civic Theatre's indebtedness to them. Cole's terse response, dated June 17, 1938, clearly shows the business side of Cole's nature, probably learned at his grandpa's knee:

> As regards the Shuberts, and your fund deficiency, I regret that I have no authority and can do nothing to help you. I have suggested numerous times to the Shuberts that they communicate with you in regard to this matter and if they have failed to do so, I can offer no further solution. Goodbye and again, many, many thanks.
>
> Sincerely,
> Cole Porter

As far as Cole Porter was concerned the matter was closed, and he turned his full attention to the opening of the much-revised *You Never Know*, starring Clifton Webb, Lupe Velez, and Libby Holman (who had rejoined the cast for the New York opening) at the Winter Garden Theatre on September 21, 1938.

You Never Know, in addition to the talents of Cole Porter, had a book adapted by Rowland Leigh and George Abbott from a play by Siegfried Geyer. The Vinton Freedly production concerns a valet masquerading as his master, and the master (Clifton Webb) tip-toes through the part of the gentleman's gentleman. The European story line and Porter's tunes just did not hit the right note with the critics or public.

The New Yorker: I wish I didn't have to write about *You Never Know* because it is sad to see so many handsome and talented people wandering helplessly around a stage. Clifton Webb, when not urbanely reciting lines that must bore him close to madness, dances stylishly as ever. Libby Holman, though

120

given practically nothing to sing, can still make my hair stand up when she digs her feet in and lets go. Cole Porter's music and lyrics only occasionally suggest that intricate and fascinating gift, and once I thought I heard the chorus sing, "Boy, it's the cats!" a line I would almost as readily have credited to Edna St. Vincent Millay.

KATE PORTER: I think a lot of the times Cole's words aren't as good as his tunes. But of course he has to write the words for the shows like they want him to.

You Never Know closed after only seventy-eight performances. It was Clifton Webb's final appearance on Broadway. He left for Hollywood and a highly successful career in Tinseltown.

COLE PORTER: It was the worst show with which I was ever connected.

The [next] show was called *Leave It to Me.* It starred Victor Moore and Sophie Tucker. June Knight, a charming singer, had one of the most prominent numbers of the score, a tune called "My Heart Belongs to Daddy." We felt that she—being in love herself with a Texas millionaire [Arthur Cameron] at the time— would give it the requisite punch. Suddenly she married the man and retired from the stage. We were vis-a-vis auditions.

An agent called me and said he had a client who might fit the role. I asked them up to the Ritz Tower and he appeared, leading a dreary little girl who appeared to be the last word in scared dowdiness. My pianist played and she sang. I must confess that such a moment is marked with five stars in my head. It was the finest audition I have ever heard. "Dress her up!" I cried. A star was born named Mary Martin. From that time forward, she sailed full steam ahead. Her voice and charm have been national assets ever since.

BELLA SPEWACK: It was the strangest audition. Cole said "Divine!" I didn't know if he meant it. So I asked her to audition in a theater so I could listen from the balcony. But before she could answer, Cole said "Deck her out," and I knew he meant he liked her.

MARY MARTIN: Sweet, swinging "Il Bacio" took me to Broadway, but it was Cole Porter's "My Heart Belongs to Daddy" that kept me there.

When I first sang "Daddy" it never entered my mind that this was a risque song. It entered a lot of other people's minds, though, or I would never have gotten the part.

I was sent to the Ritz Towers to an audition. Rosa Rio, my accompanist and I went up in an elevator halfway to heaven, into a huge living room with people sitting around in a circle like an Indian powwow. I marched in and announced, "I would like to sing four numbers. If I can't sing all four, I'd rather not sing." Get me! I was so accustomed to being stopped after one song that I was prepared to fight.

A man reclining on a couch said, very mildly, "Carry on all fours." The man on the couch who said "carry on" was Cole Porter.

I recall that when I was told that my original big number in the show had been taken out because it was not Mr. Porter's number—everything else in the show was his—I was devastated. I was so furious. I was convinced that was the song that was going to make me famous. But then it all came together when I was given "My Heart Belongs to Daddy."

LINDA PORTER: When June Knight left the show during rehearsals, a friend introduced me to a totally unknown performer. It worked out, for from the moment that Coley heard her sing, he fell in love with her and her professional manner.

Cole was too ill to attend the New Haven premiere on October 13, 1938, but Linda went. Following the final curtain call, she called him to rave about Mary Martin's performance. The way she sang "My Heart Belongs to Daddy," accompanied by a half-innocent striptease, stopped the show. Cole became so excited by what he had heard from Linda and the out-of-town press that he went up to Boston, against Dr. Moorhead's objections. The entire cast was astonished to see Cole being wheeled into one of the theater's boxes. This determination on his part brought out the best in every cast member. By February 1939, just three months after making her debut in New York, Mary Martin received featured billing in the show.

From the moment it opened at the Imperial Theatre on November 9, 1938, *Leave It to Me* was a hit. It was the highest-priced tariff of the season at $6.50 per ticket. In addition to Victor Moore, William Gaxton, Sophie Tucker, and Mary Martin, the cast was rounded out with Tamara, Edward H. Robins, and April.

The decline in Cole Porter's creative powers that had occurred after his majestic *Anything Goes* had finally been reversed.

Brooks Atkinson/*The New York Times:*** Something constructive towards the merriment of a season or so has been done in the production of *Leave It to Me!* which opened at the Imperial Theatre last evening. It is a handsome carnival which the Spewacks [Bella and Sam] have worked up from a little old 1932 rag called "Clear All Wires" and for which Cole Porter has written his wittiest score. . . .

If Mr. Porter were not at the top of his form, the performers would probably have less of the grand manner. But he has written a score that is never routine for a moment—swift, smart and ingenious, and his lyrics sparkle. . . .

Robert Benchley/*The New Yorker:* If I were a music critic, I would say that Cole Porter's music was "interesting" rather than catchy. He seems to have been concerned with writing "in the manner of" the various nations concerned, but I suppose there is no harm in that. His lyrics are in his best, which means his most you-know-what, vein, and the combination of Miss [Sophie] Tucker singing "Most Gentlemen Don't Like Love" and Miss [Mary] Martin singing "My Heart Belongs to Daddy" is one to bring a sly leer to the most bilious eye, besides representing two of the most expertly executed numbers in town.

George Jean Nathan/*Newsweek:* Cole Porter's melodies are among his very best and some of his lyrics—notably "I'm Taking the Steps to Russia," "Most Gentlemen Don't Like Love," "From Now On," and "My Heart Belongs to Daddy"— have a lot of smart fun in them.

Leave It to Me brought Cole Porter together for the first time with the husband-and-wife writing team of Sam and Bella Spewack. It was Bella to whom Cole related best, with her great instinct for musical theater and her single-mindedness about what she believed. This single-mindedness would prove useful in later years, when Bella had to convince a very reluctant Cole that he was the only composer capable of doing justice to the Spewacks' *Kiss Me, Kate.*

Despite the discovery that Cole had osteomyelitis, an inflammation of the bone marrow that made full recovery almost impossible, Cole and Linda spent Christmas of 1938 in Cartagena, Colombia. The time spent in the sun had the desired effect of giving Cole a brief period for renewal and allowing time away from his arduous work schedule.

7

"Don't Fence Me In"

THE DECADE OF the thirties gave way to the forties and, along with the desire to minimize the tragedy of his accident, there was a need at this time to look ahead.

In spite of his crippling accident, the public Cole Porter appeared to be a man ten years younger than his actual forty-nine years. He still continued to be seen at fashionable restaurants and chic private gatherings both in New York and Hollywood, whenever his health permitted.

By contrast, Linda's physical condition deteriorated. Though she was still a handsome woman, always dressed in elegant, understated clothes, at fifty-six Linda clearly showed her age. Her illness, diagnosed as emphysema, plus the passage of time had taken their toll in terms of both energy and overall appearance. The classic face that had captivated the Duke of Alba in younger days had been replaced by considerably broader features, her nose now wider and far longer than before. Her figure was no longer willowy, but that of a well-groomed dowager. Shrinking in size each year, Linda, who had been taller than Cole at the time of their marriage, was now a few inches shorter than her husband. And her bedroom was never without oxygen tanks.

As the decade was ending, Cole concluded his most productive period with just as much optimism as when it had begun. Unlike songwriters who composed over a piano keyboard, Cole stayed away from the piano until he had written the words and music of a song in his head and had put them down on paper. Then he would play it and sing it, making changes as he went along. He played with a cheerful and rhythmic shrug of his right shoulder that suggested at times a spicy "Life Is Just a Bowl of Cherries" piano player.

He had various approaches to the way he sang, too. If pleased with a lyric, he sang it with a gusto that was wonderful to witness, throwing his head back and closing his eyes (very reminiscent of "Hutch" Hutchinson). If still not too certain about the composition, he leaned forward and listened to each word as it came out of him. His singing voice was somewhat high and slightly metallic. His own comment regarding it summed it up perfectly: "I sing unpleasantly."

And when he found things did not go right or work was getting tedious, Cole always had the good sense to put things aside and socialize with his friends.

LUCIUS BEEBE: It was as a restaurant/bar that "21" had its primary reason for existence, but its fame derived from the fact that its modest facade concealed a celebrity hideaway.... If you stepped into the bar to see who was on the premises one noon in the late thirties, one or rather two of the first things you would see would be the twin beards, red and gray respectively, of Ernest Boyd, litterateur and boulevardier extraordinaire, and Edgar Montillion Woolley, director of the production *Fifty Million Frenchmen* and theater celebrity of the first order. If he was in town, Cole Porter, composer of innumerable hit songs, would be with Mr. Woolley, seated at the bar.

IN THE SPRING of 1939, on the advice of Dr. Moorhead, Cole, his valet, Paul Sylvain, and male nurse Ray Kelly set out on an arduous journey to the ruins of Machu Picchu, the Lost City of the Incas, hidden almost eight thousand feet up in the Peruvian Andes. This was an extremely ambitious and courageous undertaking for a man in his condition. His legs were still in braces, and he had to be lifted to the back of a horse, after which the group made its way up the rocky mountain paths. The areas around the ruins provided only meager accommodations, but Cole enjoyed roughing it and went out to sightsee using only his canes. Ultimately, the trip had the desired effect—Cole came back ready to take on two or three new projects.

Linda, meanwhile, had gone to Paris to close the house at 13 rue de Monsieur and, in a move designed to please her husband, had most of the furnishings shipped to California, where she had leased two houses belonging to Richard Barthelmess. The larger one was for the two of them and the smaller Malibu beach house was to be used by Cole as a work studio and retreat where he could more easily take in the sun and sea air.

During the late summer of 1939, Cole was busily writing the score for MGM's *Broadway Melody of 1939* at the Malibu beach house. The film took so long to complete that MGM was forced to retitle it *Broadway Melody of 1940.* Though the story line of this show was forgettable, the lavish "Begin the Beguine" dance sequence with Fred Astaire and Eleanor Powell was not. This number from the stage *Jubilee* was given a spirited and colorful rendition in the film. Cole's "I Concentrate on You" from the same show also became a classic.

Completing work on the film score, Cole left California for New York, having agreed to begin work on a new musical—*Du Barry Was a Lady*—brought to him by Louis Shurr and producer-songwriter-scriptwriter B. G. "Buddy" De Sylva.

LOUIS SHURR: Write it [*Du Barry*] for Ethel Merman, and I'll get you Cole Porter.

ALFRED DE LIAGRE, JR.:   Cole Porter regarded Ethel Merman above all performers in the American musical theatre. She, like Cole, was a perfectionist and had so much energy. Add to that the way she delivered a lyric. All of that appealed to him.

COLE PORTER: De Sylva called me and said he was scared of the show without a moment of low sentiment in it; I said I would write a song for it. With my tongue in cheek, I composed a ditty called "Friendship." It was one of the hits of the musical, as sung between Ethel Merman and Bert Lahr. It was nonsense and the public loved it.

MARGARET CASE HARRIMAN: He wrote "I Get a Kick Out of You" for Ethel Merman, in *Anything Goes*, when he discovered that her best notes were A-flat, B-flat, and C-natural, and that she had an engaging manner of throwing herself away in the last few bars of a song. He liked to add a few extra bars, or "tag," to a Merman chorus, holding some of the notes twice as long as usual, because he knows that Miss Merman can deliberately flat a long note and make it sound brassy and fine, and that she can work up to an exciting finish with a few unexpected bars. He tries, too, to put the words "very" and "terrific" in the lyrics he writes for Miss Merman. No one, he says, can sing these words as she can.

Time: Ethel Merman's pronunciation of show-business English brands her unmistakably as a native of parts not far from Times Square.

ARTURO TOSCANINI: She does not possess a voice but another instrument in the band.

MONTY WOOLLEY: Cole called me from Boston during the try-outs for *Du Barry Was a Lady* to inform me that he and Herbert Fields felt that my talents would fit nicely into it. When I inquired just what they had in mind they both got on the phone, and with gales of laughter coming over the telephone Cole said, "A whoremonger."

    Du Barry Was a Lady rolled into the 46th Street Theatre on December 6, 1939, after tryouts in both New Haven and Boston. It had the distinction of being the final musical comedy to premiere in the thirties, thus closing out a period that saw Cole Porter become the most popular composer of witty and sophisticated lyrics of the decade. This was his most productive period. He was at the height of his powers as a lyricist and composer, and reviewers and the public for the most part responded accordingly. Walter Winchell, who never failed to publicize Cole and his shows, reported that "they were offering $70 for a pair of opening night *Du Barry* ducats around the Stork Club." The musical outgrossed any other show in town and eventually racked up a run of 408 performances.

JOHN LAHR: The musical [*Du Barry*] had a golden ring to it. . . . Cole Porter, the Alexander Pope of American musical comedy, created the lyrics whose complexity captured the veneer and exuberance of a world as confident in its coherence as the heroic couplet.

Brooks Atkinson/*The New York Times:*   According to the title, *Du Barry Was a Lady.* As a matter of fact, she is Ethel Merman, which is more to the point, and Louis is Bert Lahr, which puts us all one up on history. As the musicmaker, Mr. Porter has written a number of accomplished tunes in the modern idiom, and one excellent romantic song, "Do I Love You?" But the lyrics are no more inspired than the book; they treat all humor as middling.

Robert Benchley/*The New Yorker:* It was a pretty tough assignment for a show as vulnerable as *Du Barry Was a Lady* to come into town with advance publicity comparable only to that accorded each year to Christmas Day. Mr. Cole Porter has come through with one of his excellent scores, the virtue of which can be more clearly estimated when they strike the radio and dance orchestras without the necromancy of Miss Merman, Miss Betty Grable, and Mr. Lahr.

George Jean Nathan/*Newsweek:* A frankly and brazenly vulgar show from start to finish, full of lavatory, boudoir and posterior gags, it may conceivably offend the delicate sensibilities of the more punctilious ladies and gents, but it is good for a lot of loud low laughs from the rest of us muckers. Mr. Porter's big song hit, "Do I Love You," may find you simultaneously whistling "It's a Long Way to Tipperary" without anyone being the wiser.

COLE PORTER: George Jean Nathan wouldn't recognize "The Star Spangled Banner" unless he saw everyone else standing up.

JOHN LAHR: When Bert Lahr first heard the *Du Barry* score, he was not immediately convinced of its excellence. The fault was quite possibly in Cole Porter's piano playing. Cole was a horrible piano player. He played with a slow, wooden tempo and if you didn't know who it was, you'd have thought he was a beginner.

If the first full orchestra rehearsal proved that Lahr's fears about the music were groundless, Porter's bitchy, urbane lyrics raised another problem. His songs were riotously funny, but they contained bawdy overtones. Although Lahr appeared to be wild and spontaneous on stage, a sense of decorum modified his antics. The clown always had to please the audience and Lahr was always conscious of creating "sympathy" on stage; as a result, he balked at some of Porter's words.

WHILE THE OPINIONS of the critics were divided on Cole Porter's latest Broadway offering, the opinion of his doctors was unanimous in that he could slowly return to a more normal schedule in his private life.

This signaled, on a very limited basis, a return to his favorite haunts in Harlem. Again, I am indebted to Monty Woolley for a post-accident look at Cole Porter and his companions trying to recapture "The Happy Heaven of Harlem."

As recounted earlier by Monty Woolley and quite accidentally confirmed a decade later by Lil Hardin Armstrong* (a friend of Clint Moore), Moore always held court in his ornate office, an exact replica of the library at France's Malmaison. Armchairs of lacquered and gilded wood were set in the curves of the back piece—two white swans with long tapering wings, their thin necks inlaid with jewel patterns. The swan theme was repeated in the upholstery of the chairs, and mahogany and bronze commodes and consoles added to the total Empire look. Moore himself, when receiving guests, was always seated behind a reproduction of a First Empire desk (the original is in Empress Josephine's study at Malmaison)—a glory in bronze and mahogany set off by the mahogany sofas that were everywhere. The top of his desk was set off by objects sent to him from around the world by grateful clients and, the most important appointment on the desk, a copy of the New York Social Register. (With his client roster, Moore had little need of the Manhattan telephone directory.)

---

*Lil Armstrong was the second wife of Louis Armstrong and a well-known jazz pianist and bandleader in her own right. Late in life, Lil entertained friends in her Chicago home at intimate but lively Sunday dinner parties, where she would recall her days in Harlem and the international jazz world. She had only one rule at these gatherings: no women guests.

Moore had his regular clients gather in the main drawing room of the house, where the young men of the house lounged around in the only clothes permitted them—loose-fitting white terry cloth robes with a large "M" embroidered on the breast pockets. The youthful studs were encouraged to keep conversation with prospective clients to a minimum while on display and were permitted to drink only a non-alcoholic fruit punch—Clint Moore believed that alcohol cut down on sexual performance.

During those years, Monty and Cole, often in the company of an old friend from Cole's Venetian period, John C. "Jack" Wilson (Noel Coward's onetime lover and theatrical producer), would run up to Harlem and spend an evening at Clint Moore's establishment. Woolley maintained that Cole, as a result of his injuries, was not always up to performing with the young men as well as he had in the years prior to his accident. On those occasions, Woolley and Cole and occasionally Wilson would repair to Cole's favorite bedroom in the Moore house.

Woolley, whose own social and personal life was always a total shambles, had the clearest memory when recalling his gamboling with Cole Porter. He described the bedroom as an exact replica of Madame Recamier's room in her home at number 7 rue de Monte-Blanc. Mahogany raged throughout the room; pilasters, doors, and window frames were all made of that wood. The windows were set off by curtains of violet silk shot with black. Two gilded bronze swans surrounded the bed with garlands of gold flowers escaping from their beaks, and the wall behind the bed consisted of a large mirror with gold and mahogany frames.

It was one of the few rooms in the house equipped with generous peepholes, placed there, of course, to observe the action in the adjoining room. Woolley explained that the action he and Cole would observe was not always between one of the studs and a customer, but rather sexual "training" sessions between an older stud and one of the younger boys. These younger trainees, usually after serving a year or two as servants at the house doing all the chores usually performed by a maid, were expected upon reaching the age of fifteen to join the ranks of the male prostitutes giving satisfaction to Clint Moore's international roster of clients.

Woolley told this writer more than once that it was the all-male sex shows that gave him and Cole and their guests their greatest pleasure. If he and Cole decided to stay the night, any youth that caught their eye during the sex show would be dispatched quickly to their individual rooms to spend the night with the two Broadway celebrities.

As the fame of Clint Moore's establishment and his reputation for having the most outstanding and reliable house of male prostitution in America spread beyond the New York/Hollywood axis, he began to "integrate" a mix of Brazilian and Puerto Rican studs into his collection. This way, said Monty, not only was he able to better satisfy regular clients like Cole and his friends, but he could also provide an ethnic mix to his famed house. This added attraction appealed to the phalanx of diplomats and foreign dignitaries from Europe and Latin America who had become an important part of his business.

Woolley also described how joyous the morning after often turned out, with Clint Moore donning a chef's hat and white apron to cook up a batch of eggs and corned beef hash for his favored guests, who washed it all down with the preferred Perrier-Jouët.

By the mid-forties, the joys of Harlem were only a memory. World War II not only depleted the supply of virile young studs so necessary to Moore's business; it brought a more prosperous air to Harlem and inspired in many of its citizens a desire for more solid achievement and less dependence on the reputation the neighborhood had as the pleasure palace of others.

That same time frame would see Cole Porter achieve in number, if not always critical success, the record that he had set in the thirties—five major Broadway shows in a row—*Panama Hattie, Let's Face It, Something for the Boys, Mexican Hayride,* and *Seven Lively Arts.*

"From This Moment On"

IN JANUARY 1940, Cole and Linda, along with their friend Leonard Hanna, journalist Bill Powell, Cleveland columnist Windsor French, and pianist Roger Stearns sailed on the S.S. *Kungsholm* for Cuba, the Panama Canal, Mexico, and the South Seas. For Cole, the Canal was a must since he was about to begin work with Herbert Fields and Buddy de Sylva on another raunchy show, *Panama Hattie*.

This trip, like all of Cole's travels, afforded him an opportunity to observe the sights and sounds of exotic places that found their way into so much of his music. Everything on the face of the earth held an interest for him. He climbed steep hills and rode far into the interior; whether the day was scorching hot or was raining torrents, Cole let nothing deter him in his quest of an ancient ruin or obscure tribal group. His special delight was flora and fauna, and he would drive miles to have a look at an unusual shrub or an animal about to become extinct. From early childhood he had been fascinated by rare bird sounds, and on one of his journeys he learned of a bird called a kling-kling that inhabited the tropical divi-divi tree, and thus was born his "The Kling-Kling Bird on the Divi-Divi Tree."

THIS TRIP ALSO provided for a significant decision in the Porters' lives, the need to secure a base of operation for them both. All thoughts of divorce had vanished, brought on in large measure by Cole's accident and the realization that though each of them needed the other, they would strike a bargain and stay married but whenever possible live and lead separate lives. They maintained separate apartments on the same floor of the Waldorf Towers. In the Brentwood, California, house, the Porters had separate suites and when in California with Linda, Cole spent as much time as possible at his Malibu beach retreat. They had never been a married couple in the conventional sense, and now that Linda was an aging matron with ongoing health problems, she wasn't seen as often on the arm of the still youthful and debonair composer. More often than not Cole escorted a bevy of society and show business beauties—Sylvia Ashley, Merle Oberon, Mary Pickford, and Dickie Fellowes-Gordon. The Porters' life together had always been an "arrangement," but at this point in their lives Linda was withdrawing far more into the background.

The decision that Linda came to on the S.S. *Kungsholm* trip was based on her reasoning that the rootlessness that resulted when she closed their Paris home of twenty years was altering the delicate balance that held their extraordinary marriage together. Despite her gradual withdrawal from high society, Linda insisted on keeping up the appearances of married life. She had, prior to the trip, investigated Long Island, but nothing there suited her. Newport had been considered and rejected. During the cruise, French suggested Williamstown, Massachusetts, and Linda thought this location had a good deal of merit, even though Cole opposed it on the grounds that possible gasoline rationing made the location totally impractical. But Linda promised French she would take a look at the college town herself.

After the voyage, one summer day in June 1940, Linda set out for Williamstown accompanied by Windsor French. None of

(above) Who, Where, and When? A photo taken about 1899 of Cole (front row, third from right) and grade school classmates. (*Miami County Historical Society*)

(left) James Omar Cole, Cole's grandfather and patriarch of the family. (*Miami County Historical Society*)

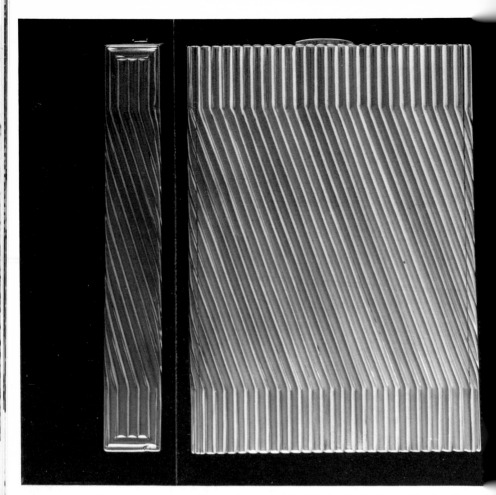

Two examples of opening night gifts to Cole from Linda: these gold boxes are set with sapphires (blue was Linda's favorite color) and were ordered from Cartier in Paris. *(Courtesy Cartier.)*

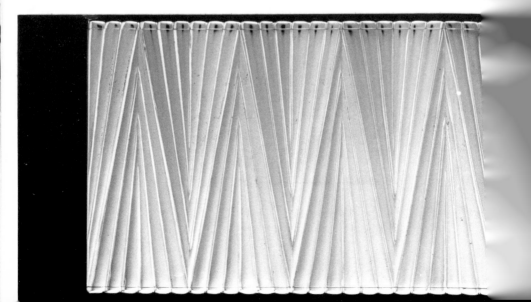

Linda Lee Porter is shown in the last decade of her life in this picture taken at the Waldorf Towers, wearing the understated attire typical of Park Avenue socialites of the period. Just a glimmer of her great beauty remains. (*The Cole Porter Collection*)

Gwen Verdon, French star Lilo, and Cole rehearsing the numbers for *Can-Can*. Once reviews were in for this show, Miss Verdon became an overnight sensation on Broadway. *(Theatre Collection, Museum of the City of New York)*

A world-weary Cole Porter posed in front of a blow-up of the score for the title song from the show *Silk Stockings. (Theatre Collection, Museum of the City of New York)*

(above) The library of Cole's nine-room Waldorf Towers apartment designed by Billy Baldwin. The highlight of this room was the tortoise-shell leather walls and bookcases with brass tubing. *(The Cole Porter Collection)*

(right) Cole and his beloved schipperke, Pepi, a gift from Merle Oberon. *(Yale University)*

In May 1957 a tired and drawn Cole Porter returns to Venice for the last time. *(AP/Wide World Photos)*

This simple headstone marks the grave of Cole Porter. He lies buried between his mother's and Linda's graves in Mount Hope Cemetery, Peru, Indiana. (*Courtesy David Grafton*)

the houses they saw appealed to them and they were about to leave when the local real estate agent suggested they take a look at Buxton Hill. For Linda, it was love at first sight. The property consisted of a large, ivy-covered fieldstone house and guest house surrounded by two-hundred acres of beautiful and meticulous lawns and gardens. Prior to making final arrangements, however, the always practical Linda decided to rent the house for a season.

Nestled in the Berkshire Mountains of western Massachusetts, Williamstown is a small New England town that was and still is charming, historic, picturesque, and all those other adjectives that seem so appropriate to this area of the nation. It is also the home of prestigious Williams College.

Cole's longtime friends Buddie and Brooke Marshall had a home nearby. Norman Rockwell lived in nearby Stockbridge; the area inspired many of his mom-and-apple-pie visions of America. Tanglewood, in neighboring Lenox, is the summer home of the Boston Symphony Orchestra and the Berkshire Theatre Festival. The entire area offered a vast potpourri for Cole and Linda and their worldly guests, and in the years to come, the Porters would visit Buxton Hill the year around.

To Buxton Hill, Linda brought her exquisite taste and some of the furniture and art objects that had been in storage from 13 rue Monsieur. It was the ultimate in urbane taste transported to a pastoral paradise.

Cole refused to be a party to the negotiations and distracted himself by driving across the northern United States and Canada, accompanied only by his valet. Upon his return, he was still not convinced about the move; it had a great deal to do with the show-business side of his nature. He was a true vagabond, always ready to experience the joys of new places and new people. It was this mix that stimulated him, and nothing as stolid as a house in the country could have the same effect.

Linda, on the other hand, needed roots. She needed her own

place, as evidenced by the first thing she did with her divorce settlement from Ned Thomas; she bought her first Paris house.

Buxton Hill, and especially the guest cottage, became a treasured retreat. With the assistance of their friend, interior designer Billy Baldwin, Linda imaginatively converted the cottage into a workplace for Cole. This small cottage was off limits to everyone except those specifically invited by Cole. To reinforce the privacy, he had a No Trespassing mat placed at the entrance to the tiny cottage; as a result, the retreat became known as "No Trespassing."

MID-SEPTEMBER OF 1940 found Cole back in New York, deep in rehearsals for *Panama Hattie*. The show starred Ethel Merman in her first role as solo star, and featured Rags Ragland, Arthur Treacher, Betty Hutton, Pat Harrington, and eight-year-old actress Joan Carroll. The plot concerns a virtuous woman who wins a good man's love against embarrassing obstacles, while also thwarting designs against the fortification of the Canal Zone. All this had a fair share of lewd jokes, with heavy doses of burlesque, and just enough patriotism to appeal to an America worried about the war in Europe.

Panama Hattie opened on October 30, 1940, at the 46th Street Theatre and received far greater acclaim than *Du Barry*. It ran 501 performances and was the show that put La Merman permanently in the ranks of Broadway stars and in the heart of every Broadway first-nighter. This was the same singer who, when George Gershwin begged her to take a singing lesson, refused. Her reply: "I breathe when I want to."

Cole Porter's shows were notable for often being the funniest and most risque in the business, and *Hattie* was no exception. This, combined with witty lyrics, guaranteed that it would prove to be the hit of the season.

IRVING BERLIN: It's worth the price of admission to hear Cole Porter's lyrics.

Brooks Atkinson/*The New York Times:* Everything is in order in *Panama Hattie,* which opened at the Forty-Sixth Street Theatre last evening. Cole Porter wrote the music and lyrics in his pithiest style and Ethel Merman sings them like a high compression engine. Cole plus Merman is a combination that has yielded some memorable musical shows in recent years. *Panama Hattie* holds her own with any of them.

JOHN O'HARA: Who would have thought we'd live to see the day when Cole Porter—Cole Porter!—would write a score in which two outstanding songs are called "My Mother Would Love You" and "Let's Be Buddies"? And written straight, too; no kidding. Ah well, he had a bad riding accident a year or two ago.

COLE PORTER: I took a tip from Buddy De Sylva's instinct for sentiment and agreed with him that a composition to diddle the public into tears would be useful at the box office. I wrote a tune called "Let's Be Buddies." Sung by Merman to a rather annoying brat, it was hogwash but it made the box office dizzy for a year.

LOUIS SOBOL: For terseness only one natural figure was more of a problem to newspaper men than the late Calvin Coolidge.

Despite this assessment by Broadway columnist Sobol, Cole expressed himself quite openly during this same period to an interviewer:

COLE PORTER: What have I got out of life? Happiness for the most part and an income which has pleased me. People have called me bittersweet, gay, off-color, complicated and eccentric. I believe that my work is simply matching mood and color to the texture of plot. If anything, I am a self-adopted Latin and my songs are derived from the sultry, disillusioned Southern hemisphere.

I am happiest when working alone on a new score with pad and pencil and rhyming dictionary. Next to that, I like to work with young people, the only continual challenge in our world. Dancers better than any, possibly because they are the most joyous. They have no thought of the future; they are always healthy without fear or care.

JULIE WILSON: Porter gives you more to work with than most songwriters. You can go anywhere you want with his songs. I wish I had the tune to get all the meaning out of the things he's done—he could make you feel so many different ways.

WITH THE ACCLAIM of *Hattie* ringing in his ears, Cole turned his attention to Columbia Pictures' *You'll Never Get Rich,* which was to star Fred Astaire and Harry Cohn's latest discovery, Rita Hayworth.

Cole expressed himself on the upcoming project in a letter to his music editor, Dr. Albert Sirmay.

June 23, 1941

Dear Doctor:

I am sending you the proofs of "Dream Dancing" and "So Near and Yet So Far," which I have corrected the best I can. But, Oh God! How it bored me. Two more proofs have just arrived, and as soon as I can bear to, I shall correct them and return them to you. Thank you so much for the clippings. It is heaven here and seems incredible that people are willing to stay in New York when it is so simple to come to California. Why on earth do you do it? I'm working very hard and believe I have some good new numbers. In any case, it's a most interesting job.

Cole Porter

When working with Cole, Dr. Sirmay would sit at one of the twin pianos in Porter's Waldorf Towers apartment, play along with Cole, and also write down the notes in a copybook. Dr. Sirmay would play it back to Cole who would make the necessary comments as to just what should be emphasized, and when the composer was finally satisfied, the song would be notated to reflect his wishes. It would then be ready for publication.

AMERICA WAS NOW at war. Cole Porter's contribution added up to a few appearances at various charity benefits hosted by such friends as Mrs. Lytle Hull, Mrs. William Randolph Hearst, Sr., and Elsa Maxwell. From time to time he would gather up a group of young servicemen from the various service centers around New York and in the company of Monty Woolley take them to the most expensive restaurants in the city. It was his way of showing them a good time, at the same time exposing him to a new crop of young men, all the while doing his "patriotic duty."

The war had an effect on Cole's East-West Coast travel; formerly he had used ships and trains the way people now use jets. With troop trains making luxury travel a thing of the past, Cole whenever possible would fly back and forth between New York and California. Occasionally, if he was able to get enough gasoline in gas-rationed America, he would drive between the coasts.

Prior to the war the Porters traveled like visiting royalty, he with a valet, she with a maid, and they shared the services of a maid whose sole duty was to press their clothes. On trains they would sometimes take an entire car for themselves, their mountain of luggage, and—always—a large group of friends. The same would hold true when traveling aboard ships; three or four cabins would be booked for the Porters and another group of cabins for friends who traveled the globe with them.

On the occasions that Cole did take the train from New York to California, he would board the 20th-Century Limited at Grand Central Station in Manhattan, arrive in Chicago the next day just in time to lunch in Booth Number One in that city's famed Pump Room, and then entertain aboard the famous Super Chief. Yale classmate and railroad tycoon W. Averell Harriman saw to it that Cole had the best accommodations possible despite the overcrowding on all trains in wartime America. But once Cole began to use airplanes on a regular basis, it soon became his favorite mode of transportation. And with his physical condition, flying meant that his infirmity was not aggravated by long journeys.

DESPITE A BRIEF period of depression, triggered far more by his precarious physical condition than anything to do with the vagaries of Hollywood moguls, Cole pepped up considerably when Dorothy Fields and her brother Herbert arrived to begin work with him on the upcoming Broadway musical *Let's Face It.* When he learned that Danny Kaye would star, he was euphoric.

In addition to Kaye, the cast included Eve Arden, Benny Baker, Vivian Vance, Mary Jane Walsh, and Nanette Fabray.

When the new Porter show arrived at the Imperial Theatre on October 29, 1941, the reviews were excellent and the public went wild over Danny Kaye's performance, which in large measure accounted for the show's run of 547 performances.

The New York Times: Cole Porter has shaken some good tunes and rhymes out of his sophisticated juke-box.

For let's face the eerie fact, the songs are designed for enjoyment. "Jerry, My Soldier Boy" is resounding band music. "You Irritate Me" is "You're the Top" turned upside down. In "Farming," Mr. Porter shakes a wry stick at the sport of smart people.

"Let's Not Talk About Love" restores the Porter song to its ancient eminence as a test of memory and wind.

The New Yorker: Cole Porter's music and lyrics, though containing some echoes from the master's previous works, are very pleasant and witty, and several of them, like "Everything I Love" and "Farming," are probably even better than that.

COLE PORTER: The opening was one of the most polished and winning of any of my shows (with the hit called "Everything I Love"). Kaye has since gone on to even greater heights but he still retains all his original naivete. I often think of him with terror as an innocent lost in the maze of his own virtuosity.

DOROTHY KILGALLEN: Cole Porter walked into the Colony the other night with almost no limp at all, which is such good news after all he's been through.

AS IN THE past, the popularity of *Let's Face It* had a decided tonic effect on Cole's spirits at a time in his life when periods of depression were very noticeable. With the glowing reviews in his pocket, Cole set out for Hollywood in the spring of 1942 with a commitment from Columbia to score a film, even though a commitment and a contract from the volatile Hollywood studio bosses often did little more than announce their desire to do a project. The studio moguls had contempt for everyone on their studio roster, and contracts were signed and projects dropped on a whim.

All that Cole knew about the film as he arrived in California aboard the 20th-Century was that the cast would be headed by William Gaxton, Don Ameche, Janet Blair, and Jack Oakie. The following wire from the director, Russian-born actor-turned-producer-and-director Gregory Ratoff, showed just how things were done in Tinseltown:

> Will you write a very optimistic song under the title "Something to Shout About"? This will be the stock phrase of Billy Gaxton as a producer. All through the picture he will be saying, "I want the kind of show that there'll be something to shout about." Columbia sales organization here begs me to call the picture *Something to Shout About*. They know the pulse of the picture-going public and they are always looking for a saleable title.

Naturally Cole complied and gave Ratoff and the studio just what they wanted. As so often happens, the title tune failed to catch on with the public, but another Porter tune from the film, "You'd Be So Nice to Come Home To," as sung by Janet Blair and Don Ameche, was an instant hit with a public longing to see the loved ones they were separated from by the war.

RETURNING TO NEW York, Porter began work on his next Broadway production, again teamed with the writing duo of Herbert and Dorothy Fields. The brother-sister team took full advantage of the patriotic fervor rampant in the land and titled their new show *Something for the Boys*. This show again would be graced with the supreme talent of Ethel Merman, performing in her fifth and final Cole Porter musical. An imaginative and youthful producer named Mike Todd, who had made his mark on Broadway with an all-black cast in the 1939 production of *The Hot Mikado*, took over when Vinton Freedly quit the show after differences with Cole and the Fields. In addition to Ethel Merman, the cast included Paula Laurence, Allen Jenkins, Betty Garrett, and Betty Bruce.

Something for the Boys opened at the Alvin Theatre on January 7, 1943, and ran for 422 performances.

The New York Times: All season long the world has yearned hopefully for a big, fast, glittering musical comedy. It has it now, for last evening the fabulous Mike Todd brought in *Something for the Boys,* and as it danced its way across the stage of the Alvin it quite clearly was not only something pretty wonderful for the boys, but something for the girls as well. For Cole Porter has taken tunes from his topmost drawer, Herbert and Dorothy Fields have written words that are better than most, Hassard Short has directed in his usual impeccable manner and Ethel Merman gives a performance that suggests all Merman performances before last night were simply practice. In short, this is the musical comedy for which Broadway has been waiting a long, long time.

The New Yorker: Mr. Porter's music and lyrics are all right with me, though now and then I miss the eerie complexity of the old rhymes and even feel that the master is less inclined to be flippant about love than he was in the days when he was writing hymns to the sex life of the bean and the cod. However, such pieces as "Hey, Good Lookin'," "He's a Right Guy," and "I'm in Love with a Soldier Boy" are pretty enough for any reasonable man, and something called "By the Mississinewah," an Indian lyric of sorts executed by Miss Merman and Miss Laurence, is surely memorable enough in its queer way to trouble your dreams.

COLE PORTER: I had heard of a young and rising impresario who had just produced some Gilbert and Sullivan in swingtime, called *The Hot Mikado.* I phoned Mike Todd and told him that I was writing a show with some friends of mine and indicated that Vinton Freedly refused to continue with the production. I asked Mike Todd if he'd step in. I told him that if he'd like, we could arrange an audition. His reply was, "I don't need to hear or see anything. If you're doing the music, I'll produce it." It was a gesture so typical of the man, and the show turned out to be a success for me and all concerned.

MIKE TODD: I received an offer of $350,000 from United Artists for the screen rights to *Something for the Boys*. This bid is said to top Samuel Goldwyn's by more than $50,000.

IN EARLY SPRING 1944, Cole joined Linda at Buxton Hill, and he began work almost immediately on the score for his next Broadway outing. Life at Buxton Hill, thanks to Linda's deft touch, proved good for Cole's work and general well-being.

The day would begin with breakfast and all the New York newspapers. Walter Winchell's column in *The Daily Mirror* was always the first thing he turned to. After that he wrote in his cottage until lunchtime and often later, but always stopped in time to enjoy one of his folk heroes, NBC radio's "Stella Dallas." Cole had discovered the soap opera by accident while searching for a talk show. When Cole was on the West Coast, Stella's broadcast fell during lunch, and his guests were forbidden to speak. Those who failed to obey were not asked again. During the afternoons at Williamstown, Cole would often take a drive. But most of the time at Buxton Hill was spent working on the score for another show.

A former resident of Peru, Indiana, Maxine Fogelman Bateman, provides an insight into the composer's life at Williamstown during the wartime period:

> Dear Bob:*
>
> When you told me about your forthcoming program commemorating the life of Cole Porter, it brought to mind an interesting, and very embarrassing, experience I had with this well-known gentleman.

*Bob Smith, Peru neighbor and friend.

146

As you know, the Porters maintained a summer home in Williamstown, Mass., the site of Williams College where Dick [Richard Bateman] was stationed for 14 months during World War II. One day the telephone rang and a masculine voice announced he was Cole Porter calling to see if I would be interested in doing some secretarial work at his home during the summer. I was so certain some of my friends were pulling my leg, I immediately responded, "Oh, yes, well, this is Eleanor Roosevelt, what can I do for you?"

After a long silence, the caller insisted he was who he claimed to be and he did need a secretary. Embarrassed, I agreed to an interview, and when I arrived for it Cole was sitting by his swimming pool, his crutches nearby, and a table in front of him held many medicine bottles.

When he asked me where I was from, I answered, "Peru, Indiana." He gave me a puzzled look and answered, "Now you're pulling my leg." I assured him I wasn't, and added, "Your aunt Rachel Chalice taught me in grade school."

He hired me and I spent the entire summer, daily in the guest house of the Porter mansion working for him. My main job as a secretary seemed to be pasting his and Linda's press clippings in scrapbooks.

As a result, I was privileged to share a close association with a man I shall always remember.

Maxine

JUNE 1944 FOUND Cole and Linda in Mexico City with Mike Todd and a production staff for a projected Todd musical. At this point the show was called *Light Wines and Dancing;* it ultimately became *Mexican Hayride.*

Because he contracted dysentery, Cole was forced to leave Mexico after only two weeks. His generally run-down condition caused the osteomyelitis to flare up, resulting in further surgery at New York's Doctors' Hospital. As soon as he had recovered he entrained for Boston, where *Mexican Hayride* was in tryout. Here he found time to give the bride away at the wedding of Lieutenant Edward John, Lord Stanley, and the former Lady Sylvia Ashley. The press always preferred to refer to the Cockney-born chorus girl as Lady Ashley, despite the fact that at the time of her marriage to Lord Stanley she was the widow of Douglas Fairbanks, Sr. This radiant, blond glamour girl, a great favorite of Cole's, subsequently married Clark Gable and finally Russian-born Prince Dimitri Djordjadze, becoming the epitome of the chorus girl who made good.

Linda commissioned the Duke di Verdura to create a presentation case for Cole to mark the Boston opening of *Mexican Hayride* on December 29, 1943. This particular cigarette case was of fourteen-karat gold, and the lid was set with two gold pieces-of-eight connected by engraved ribbons, with the obverse of the coins visible on the inside of the lid.

Mexican Hayride opened at the Winter Garden in New York on January 28, 1944. Although it received unfavorable reviews, it had enough gaiety and humor to play to a packed house for months, ending its run at 481 performances. The cast was headed by comedian Bobby Clark, Wilbur Evans, June Havoc, and Luba Malina.

In July, June Havoc left the cast, ostensibly because of an injury incurred during the show. Actually, she had been offered the starring role in *Sadie Thompson,* the musical version of Somerset Maugham's *Rain.* As he had done when Mary Boland abandoned *Jubilee,* he added June Havoc's name to a growing list of performers who were never again considered for a Porter show.

The New Yorker: The great disappointment about it [*Mexican Hayride*] I think is Cole Porter's music, which is not only derivative but at the moment as non-memorable to me as the sound that goes with a hurdy-gurdy. . . .

The New York Morning Telegram: Cole Porter's talent has very nearly reached the vanishing point. . . .

COLE PORTER: *Mexican Hayride* I never liked—it was memorable to me for a bet I made with Monty Woolley.

While *Mexican Hayride* was still in tryout in Boston, Monty challenged Cole to write a hit song titled "I Love You," in which that hackneyed phrase would be repeated over and over. Monty felt that even given Cole's great talent and gift for words and music, he would not be able to surmount such a hindrance. To back up the challenge, Woolley laid down a small wager of $5. Always up to a challenge, especially from Monty, Cole came up with a rather listless refrain. However, Wilbur Evans's big voice did much to put "I Love You" over in the show and it became a major hit, enabling Cole to win the wager.

Mike Todd sent the following telegram to Cole Porter on February 4, 1944: DEAR COLE: BING CROSBY IS RECORD-ING "I LOVE YOU" A WEEK FROM TODAY. I LOVE YOU.

Before the end of April, the Crosby recording was the best-selling record in America, while the song itself was second in nationwide sheet-music sales and number one on radio's "Lucky Strike Hit Parade."

WHILE *MEXICAN HAYRIDE* was still on Broadway, Cole's next show, *Seven Lively Arts,* opened at the Ziegfeld Theatre on December 7, 1944. This lackluster production ran only 183 performances. Produced by the flamboyant Billy Rose of Diamond Horseshoe fame, it starred Beatrice Lillie, Bert Lahr, Benny Goodman,

Alicia Markova, Anton Dolin, Dolores Gray, Teddy Wilson, and Red Norvo.

The New Yorker: Given a good deal of cutting, which oughtn't be hard, Billy Rose's *Seven Lively Arts* will probably be a very satisfactory show, though not quite warranting all the fuss that was made about its advent (admission, twenty-four dollars, champagne served in the intermission, the audience will please dress)... Cole Porter's music is pleasant enough, though not likely to haunt your dreams, and his lyrics are ingenious if occasionally a little labored.

BENNY GOODMAN: My only association with Cole was when I had a jazz group in a show by Billy Rose called *Seven Lively Arts.* I think he was one of the greatest songwriters of the ages.

COLE PORTER: At about this time I commenced to think that the rumors of Broadway about my being through may have had some substance. Linda was there to reassure me and I believed her where I believed no one else.

THIS SAME PERIOD in his career found Cole lending his hand to a western song, "Don't Fence Me In." It was a tune that he had originally written for a 1934 Twentieth Century-Fox film project that never went beyond the planning stage. At the suggestion of producer Lou Brock, a Helena, Montana, friend, Bob Fletcher, sent to Cole a book of his verse, which contained a number of poems that had appealed to the Hollywood producer. Brock encouraged his friend to write a Western tune, even suggesting that he would want the chorus to start with the words "Don't Fence Me In."

The former cowhand followed up on this suggestion, and when he finished he sent to Cole the lyrics and music for the refrain of "Don't Fence Me In" along with some music for the verse. Cole agreed to pay Fletcher $250 for all rights to his music and to attempt to see to it that Fletcher received recognition for the material. Cole packed the song with every Western cliche he could think of.

Once the song was published, there was no mention of Fletcher. Porter later made amends for the oversight and signed over a portion of the royalties from the song to Fletcher, an act of generosity that was not required of him. The unused song at Fox eventually made its way to Warner Brothers, where it was sung by Roy Rogers in the 1944 film *Hollywood Canteen,* and a best-selling record by Bing Crosby and the Andrew Sisters sent Cole's tune to the top of the Hit Parade. The sheet music and record sales both hit the one million mark.

HAZEL MEYER: All hints not withstanding, the Broadway music business paid little attention to what was a dormant trend until in 1944, Cole Porter's version of a western song—"Don't Fence Me In"—became an overnight sensation. Mr. Porter had written his song several years earlier, but it lay a-moldering on a shelf at Harms, Inc. until it was planted in a Warner Brothers film by one of Tin Pan Alley's most beloved song-pluggers, Mose Gumble.

But even the brilliant success of "Don't Fence Me In" failed to convince the industry that a significant new twang in popular music had sounded. The song was thought to be a hit because it was written by Cole Porter and given lavish production in a star-studded movie following aggressive plugging as soon as its effect on sales was noticed.

IT WAS AT this same time that Cole's great friend and fellow composer Irving Berlin suggested to Jack Warner the idea for a film biography of Cole's life.

Warner liked the idea very much, but it took time to reach an agreement that resulted in a fictionalized *Night and Day,* with Cole collecting $300,000 for the rights to his life story. The actual film deviated quite a bit from the truth. For one thing,

Porter indulged a fantasy shared by many men by insisting that Cary Grant play the lead, and the tall, handsome, fortyish Grant was totally out of place as a young Yale student singing "Bull Dog." For another, the fictional Cole Porter was portrayed as a soldier-hero during the First World War, badly wounded by an exploding bomb. The only near-plausible presence in *Night and Day* was the choice by Linda of the beautiful and elegant Alexis Smith as her film counterpart. Monty Woolley played the only part he was capable of playing—himself, but he played himself as a professor of Cole's at Yale rather than the fellow student he had been. Other cast members were Mary Martin, Jane Wyman, and Eve Arden.

LOUELLA PARSONS: What a honey of a movie Cole Porter's life should make. When I heard Jack Warner was planning a film about the famous socialite-composer I wondered how come no one had thought of the idea before. It's a natural not only because Porter's imposing array of hit tunes will provide a ready-made score, but also because his life has been full of the stuff of which stories are made.

ELSA MAXWELL: Arriving in Beverly Hills after leaving San Francisco is a transition of sharp contrast. It takes a week to acclimate yourself to a new and different world. But not when you step practically off the train into Cole Porter's lovely house and garden near Santa Monica.

For all is sweetness and light, and I found Cole brown and so much stronger after his last winter's several operations—any one of which would have floored men with less courage—in the Doctors' Hospital.

Cole was in great form and there were three tables of eight lining the swimming pool, with a barbecue where his cook was grilling meat, which after so many meatless days in San Francisco seemed like a dream.

The Basil Rathbones were there. You always know hand-some Basil by his Sherlock Holmes over the radio.

Cary Grant is handsomer than ever. Then George Cukor, the director, witty and brilliant and the best director in Hollywood. Constance Collier, who is a darling, complained rather sadly that she was afraid her part in *Weekend at the Waldorf*, in which she portrayed so perfectly an ex-prima donna, was cut.

William Somerset Maugham was also a guest of Cole's. I never saw Willie look better and I never found him in better form. Jack and Ann Warner were there to greet me—Ann sweeter and more charming than ever. Jack could not eclipse Cole's check coat, striped bow tie and bold pink shirt.

Ann Warner exudes more charm from her little fingertips than all the manicured, streamlined glamour girls in Holly-wood. And when you know Hollywood, you will realize that a great deal of the direction, planning of pictures, and personali-ties who are going to appear in them is done at just such parties like this.

For example, when you say Jack Warner, Ann Warner, and Cary Grant lunched at Cole Porter's, you realize that Cole's new picture of his life, called *Night and Day*, is about to begin and as Cary Grant is going to play Cole on the screen, it is certainly a break for Cole.

JACK WARNER: (Telegram to Cole after a sneak preview of *Night and Day*): REACTION WAS EVERYTHING ONE WOULD DESIRE. WE HAVE AN IMPORTANT FILM AND ONE I KNOW YOU WILL BE VERY PROUD OF AND ALSO A SUCCESS WHICH I KNOW IS WHAT COUNTS.

COLE PORTER: (Response to Michael Curtiz after seeing the film): BELOVED MIKE, LINDA AND I SAW NIGHT AND DAY PICTURE FRIDAY NIGHT AND YOU HAVE OUR ETERNAL GRATITUDE FOR TREATING US SO BEAUTIFULLY. WHAT

A GREAT DIRECTOR YOU ARE AND HOW LUCKY WE WERE TO HAVE BEEN PUT IN YOUR HANDS.

DOUGLAS FAIRBANKS, JR.: I did know him over a number of years and I'm very proud to have been counted among his friends. My wife was also a very good friend and was devoted to him ... but I do remember there was a godawful movie, purportedly a biography, but which was certainly not a recognizable account of his life.

COLE PORTER'S HOLLYWOOD home was lovely, but he had to sue to keep it. The owner, actor-turned-decorator C. William Haines, asked the composer to vacate the property at the end of his year's lease. Seeking to avoid eviction from the imposing mansion at 416 North Rockingham Avenue in Brentwood Heights, Cole filed suit in Federal Court to force renewal of the lease for another year.

The composer charged in his action that Haines leased the property to him two years previously with the agreement that the lease might be renewed at the end of each year, provided written notice was given sixty days in advance. Porter asserted that he met the terms of the agreement but that Haines refused to renew the lease, contending that he did not receive such a notice.

According to the complaint, Porter was to pay $6,600 a year for the use of the property and during the two-year occupancy he had spent approximately $20,000 in improvements.

Porter asked that the court order the lease renewed. Apparently the suit was settled in Cole's favor, for the Brentwood estate became the Porter's West Coast residence for the rest of their lives.

With the box office, if not the artistic, success of *Night and Day* ringing in his ears, Cole headed east to begin work on another Broadway show, *Around the World in Eighty Days*, with Orson Welles as the director-producer as well as the lead.

<u>COLE PORTER:</u>   It might have been a success except for the fluctuating backers.

I have rarely admired a man so much. Welles did everything possible toward the success of *Around the World in Eighty Days*, going without sleep or food for one week, subsisting only on coffee.

The failure of this show was so great that my own reputation suffered mightily.

It was difficult to think of any theatrical stunt that Orson Welles had overlooked in staging Jules Verne's novel of Phileas Fogg's eighty-day race around the planet. The show was a zany Olsen-and-Johnson-*Hellzapoppin* treatment of a classic in the hands of a genius gone completely wrong.

Around the World in Eighty Days opened at the Adelphi on May 31, 1946, and ran only seventy-five performances. In addition to Welles, the cast included: Mary Healy, Larry Laurence (Enzo Stuarti), and Arthur Margetson, as the unruffled globetrotter.

The New Yorker: And if God will forgive me, Mr. Cole Porter's music and lyrics are hardly remarkable at all.

Newsweek: The score, for instance, is no more than adequate.

ROAD TRYOUTS ARE often grueling and tedious, even for those in the best of health. In order to keep his creative juices flowing, Cole found it necessary to provide himself with as many creature comforts as possible during the out-of-town tryouts.

When Cole Porter traveled to tryouts, whether in Philadelphia, Boston, or New Haven, his own ashtrays went along with him, and he liked them kept so neat that at parties in his suite, a servant emptied them out almost before a guest could crunch a cigarette out. A large Grandma Moses (his favorite artist) snowscape always accompanied him and would always be placed above the piano, making the hotel suite a little more like home.

While working on a show, he kept his music and lyrics in neat sets of looseleaf notebooks and manilla folders, and he followed a chart of the book's plot for spotting his songs. And just as in his Yale days, on top of the piano there would be a dish filled with caramels from Arnold's Candies in Peru, Indiana. Cole had a standing order at Arnold's for five pounds of the caramels to be sent each month.

At age fifty-five, the great sophisticate of international society had mellowed slightly and was thinking back more and more to his hometown roots. Madcap days in Paris and Venice were now just a fading memory. His work and the memories of unspoiled youth among kinfolk and friends increasingly occupied his thoughts.

9

"Another Op'nin', Another Show"

AND WHAT AN op'nin' and what a show! For with *Kiss Me, Kate,* Cole Porter gave the theater and the theater-going public his masterpiece.

Kate was the culmination of all his years of work in the theater and was a complete vindication of the recent past, when so many Broadway seers had predicted that Cole Porter was finished.

TOM PRIDEAUX: As the houselights at the New Century Theatre dimmed on the evening of December 30, 1948, and the conductor made his way through the orchestra pit to the podium, the spotlight that picked him out as he bowed to the elegant first-night audience also picked up an answering gleam from an aisle seat on the fourth row. It illuminated a white tie beneath a line of equally white teeth bared into an impish grin. It was the kind of tie that goes with top hat and tails, and it was worn, of course, by Cole Porter. It was the opening night of *Kiss Me, Kate,* the seventh Broadway musical for which Porter had written the songs and lyrics. The show had been an instant success during its tryout in Philadelphia. Hopeful that his recent period of producing mediocre shows was about to be ended, Porter had bought 97 seats for the Broadway opening.

He was sitting on the aisle so that he could stretch out his chronically painful right leg after the show began. His seat was on the "string side" of the orchestra because for spectators in the front rows string players were less likely to drown out the singers than the noisy brass blowers. As always, Porter was prepared to savor the performance of his own work, laughing and applauding the performers, occasionally leaning over to a companion to remark, "Isn't it great?"*

On that glorious night, Cole Porter was the picture of relaxed enjoyment and a sight to amaze his fellow composers and authors, who generally paced, squirmed, and chewed their nails backstage or in the lobby during a first performance. Playwright Russel Crouse once called Porter's composure at his own first nights as "indecent as the bridegroom who has a good time at his own wedding."

A Cole Porter first night was, in fact, a sort of ceremonial meeting of the two sides of his life—show business and the high-living, high-class international society that lionized him long before his songs received public acclaim. Between opening nights, Cole shuttled back and forth between the greasepaint world of Bert Lahr and the glittery, brittle world of Elsa Maxwell.

The opening of *Kiss Me, Kate* masked the personal heartache and the day-to-day trial and error that had preceded; it was a period of great self-doubt on all sides, especially on the part of Cole Porter, who among other things felt that he was not up to setting Shakespeare to music.

*American Musicals/*Cole Porter*, by Tom Prideaux. Copyright © 1981 by Time-Life Books, Inc.

COLE PORTER: I commenced sweating on an idea with a soap opera writer—if a notion of how desperate I was may be given—when the famous writing team of Sam and Bella Spewack came to me with the suggestion of doing Shakespeare's *Taming of the Shrew* as a musical. I swore it could not be done, whereupon they wrote a single scene. I read it, liked it, and wrote a single song. So the second great "perfect" hit was born.

BELLA SPEWACK: I wrote out suggestions for song titles to stimulate him, and it just came like an avalanche once the initial strivings were over. He started writing. He signed with the producers on March 30, and we signed our collaboration contract later. There was nothing in writing between us. We had no lawyer, and you know I don't think I could do that with anybody else. It was just Cole's word.

JACK WILSON: Who could have foreseen on the Lido in 1925, a Cole Porter *Kiss Me, Kate* staged by John C. Wilson! I am so proud and happy about it all and Cole, aside from simply being a genius, is the sweetest, kindest person in show business.

SOMETIME BEFORE BEGINNING *Kiss Me, Kate,* Cole was saddened by the death of his longtime secretary, Margaret Moore. Before long, however, he would find Madeline Smith, an equally capable secretary who, in the coming years, would prove to be a great asset to the composer.

MADELINE P. SMITH: If you choose the right boss, you might even shine by reflected glory, if you are always true to him in your fashion.

Although I can claim no credit for the choosing, I was brought to the right door, since Heaven protects the poor working girl, and I believe in Heaven. I went to New York fresh from four years at the Belgian Embassy in Washington where, as personal and social secretary to the Belgian ambassador—a rather stilted life for an American girl—it behooved me to cast around for something interesting to do and hopefully, remunerative. After an assortment of trials, Lady Ashley (who was then Mrs. Douglas Fairbanks, Sr.) came into my life and it was through her that I met the great Cole Porter.

Late one afternoon, she asked me to walk with her to the Pavillon Restaurant, where she was to meet her host for dinner. For once in her life, she planned to be on time. "I can't keep Cole Porter waiting," she said, "If I'm late I'll find him seated in the choicest table in the place beginning his dinner without me." So, having arrived before Mr. Porter, she introduced us when he came in. That was my first meeting.

No doubt she put in a good word for me (which never does any harm), for late one night not long after, he telephoned asking me if I could come down to the Waldorf to help him with some letters and lyrics. As it was 10 o'clock, I suggested that it was a bit late to start work; nevertheless, I would come down. It never occurred to him that anything he wanted or needed would not be forthcoming. I found him in a wheelchair, immaculately garbed in a white silk robe, both legs in casts, smiling gayly, with no hint of the pain that I later learned was always with him. Dinner had just been finished and his valet brought in coffee. We chatted a bit before beginning the evening's work, consisting of letters, always brief, and some lyrics for the musical *Kiss Me Kate*, on which he had just begun work.

"This man is clever," I thought to myself—and indeed he was, I found out many times over.

Now had begun my first business encounter with my boss, not that I called him that, for formality was the word all through the years. Only his devoted valet (Paul Sylvain) for 22 years referred to him as "my boss." I always addressed him as "Mr. Porter" and he called me "Mrs. Smith." Almost no one became familiar with Cole Porter. He was approached by the world at large with great deference, not only on account of his

160

tremendous talent, but because that was the kind of man he was, always polite, somewhat distant, complex, sophisticated (he hated to be called sophisticated, even though he was), widely traveled, devoted to his immediate family and his work.

He used to say, "I think so hard when I am working that I always get a headache."

I would find little slips of paper on my desk every morning, with suggestions written thereon as they came to him, advising me what I should do during the day. This was his way of freeing his mind of details so he could concentrate on his most important work. Thoughts regarding his lyrics and his music must have been running through his mind all the time, for I constantly saw penciled bars of music on scraps of paper and lists of rhyming words, eventually to be incorporated in a finished composition.

His was the one-track mind of a deep thinker. I early realized that nonessential remarks fell on deaf ears during creative spells. There was a dearth of words in all his business letters, though every word expressive, but a wealth of words in his letters to his wife and to his mother, to both of whom he was devoted.

Sly humor was ever in the background: "Spend your money, don't hide it in little bags around the house," he admonished his 81-year-old mother (whom he called "Ma" or "The Great Katie"—she died at nearly 91).

He was always concerned if any misfortune befell his family, his friends or his employees. To his wife, long an invalid, he wrote, "Linda dear, I worry if you so much as scratch your little finger." He couldn't bear to dismiss anyone from his service, even though they might be totally unworthy. Somehow, a former jailbird was unwittingly hired to serve in California and brought to New York. It was I who had to fire him!

His mother came every winter, with her faithful companion, Mrs. Lou Bearss (ex-showgirl who married into the family) and stayed in the apartment across the hall. They always accused

Mr. Porter of arranging quarters for them nearby so he could check on how late they came in nights. They stayed until springtime each year, when "The Great Katie" would become restless and announce, "I must go home now, Cole, and do my spring planting." I could visualize this little lady pushing a big plow laboriously through the fields! It was a cousin, J. Omar Cole, who managed all the family business pertaining to the farm. "You look so much younger than your cousin," I once mentioned to Mr. Porter, "and he's only six months older than you." "Oh, he was born old!" was his reply.

Over the years he traveled to Europe to be in the company of many friends, titled and otherwise. In Italy, Bernard Berenson asked him on one visit, "How old are you, Cole?" "Sixty-five," was the answer. "Oh, a mere chicken—I'm 92," replied the great art critic. In earlier days Mrs. Porter always accompanied her husband on his trips overseas. She was adored by the Duke of Alba, whom she knew before marrying Cole. "If only you were not a divorcée!" had been his sad comment. He continued his devoted friendship all through her life. Very likely she might have become the Duchess of Alba had conditions not been as they were, and had she not met Cole Porter.

There were many gay days in Paris, the Rezzonico Palazzo home in Venice (now a museum), with brilliant parties, and then the settling down in New York, followed by the Cole Porter musical comedy shows and songs known the world over. Elsa Maxwell, Anita Loos, Lady Duff-Gordon, Howard Sturges, Diana Vreeland, Baron de Gunzburg, Duc di Verdura, Duke and Duchess de Talleyrand, Mrs. Lytle Hull, Mr. and Mrs. William Rhinelander Stewart, Countess von Bismarck, Noel Coward, the Duke and Duchess of Windsor and so many of the world's best-known people crossed his threshold at one time or another.

He loved to have dinner guests, and the arranging of this turned out to be my job. I telephoned all the invitations. He

never used engraved or written invitations, always the telephone, but an engraved reminder card invariably followed. His
friends were also among the laity, people who contributed to
the interests in his life, and who could converse with him on his
own level, such as George Eells, who eventually wrote the Cole
Porter biography *The Life That Late He Led,* and Lew Kesler,
piano-conductor for the orchestra playing for most of his early
musicals, and many others who have since passed away.

Elsa Maxwell lived a few floors below him at the Waldorf. He
didn't mind using her as a sound board for jokes. "She can take
it, there's plenty of her," he said. Once he sent her half a cake
that had been given to him for Christmas. "We can't let her
starve," he commented. But when he also sent along a pound of
very expensive caviar, he was chagrined to hear her say on TV
not long afterward, "I do hate caviar!" "Next time we'll give it
to the birds," he said.

Many of his summers were spent in his Brentwood home in
Los Angeles, where the great of the theater world congregated:
director George Cukor, Louis B. Mayer, David Selznick, Moss
Hart, Mary Martin, Grace Kelly, Fred Astaire, far too many to
mention. Never a dull moment. One of his favorites was Artur
Rubinstein, to whose home he delighted to go, and where the
whole family was a joy to be with. I clipped and sent him all the
gossip columns from the New York newspapers. Each fall, on
his return to his Waldorf Towers apartment for the winter, I
took great pride in seeing that everything was shipshape
before his arrival, including fresh potpourri (which I made
myself) for all the precious bowls.

At Christmas time he was always in a quandary as to what
presents to give to his friends. I couldn't help him too much,
especially after a dozen years had gone by, for what can you
give to people who have everything? He received a mink can
opener from Mrs. Jessie Donahue (the Woolworth heiress and
aunt to Barbara Hutton), which he promptly sent on to another

"has everything" friend. He was particularly fond of playing jokes on Monty Woolley. He gave him a toy Santa Claus one Christmas with a long white cotton beard; one could blow it out of a tube and it came down in a parachute, long beard and all. He gave him a muffler "to be worn well up over the lower part of the face—it has an aversion to sarcasm," the card said (Monty was known for making sarcastic remarks).

He also bought fake jewelry at the five and dime store (I had to show him the way there, for he had never been in a Woolworth store before) to give to the lady guests at a luncheon once during the holidays. The salesgirl told him it would cost him an extra ten cents each for boxes in which to put the separate pieces. "Well, I guess that will be all right—they're expensive, aren't they?" without a smile. The girl had no idea she was talking to a millionaire as she commiserated with him on how costly everything was these days.

During the many months he had to wear casts on his legs he called them "Geraldine and Josephine," always making light of his infirmities, never dwelling on the agony with which he was so often plagued. I could not but marvel at his indomitable endurance, for his face belied his words. In spite of it all he persisted in his work and produced many of his finest works while his spirits and his physique were at their lowest. He, indeed, had the unbeatable courage.

ELISE SMITH: With *Kiss Me, Kate* that was my first night out on the town in a long dress . . . Mr. Porter decided that my whole family—my mother, my father, my brother and I—were going to the opening of *Kiss Me, Kate!* Oh, yes! I met Mrs. Kate Porter, the mother, in the early 1950s. She was a very dainty woman, very small. Mr. Porter looked very much like her; the big eyes, the dark hair.

I was sort of aware of when he had his leg amputated—I believe it was in 1959. Almost at the same time, he lost his very faithful valet, Paul Sylvain. I remember going up to visit Paul at Columbia-Presbyterian. . . . Paul had been with Mr. Porter many years, and he always referred to Mr. Porter as "The Boss. I'll do anything for the Boss." Paul was just a wonderful man.

Mr. Porter would have to have his bones scraped periodically because of the build-up of "deceased" bone tissue and for this he would go up to Columbia-Presbyterian Medical Center. Whenever he was there, he would always have people for cocktails at the hospital. Mom would make up the guest list and get in contact with people who had agreed to go up to the hospital for afternoon cocktails with Mr. Porter. She always could get someone to go up and visit him, for whatever period of time he was there. But one day, no one could make it. Mom was concerned that no one was going to see Mr. Porter so she asked me if I would go. I said OK, so I thought it would be nice to bring him a little plant or flower. I went out and bought two geraniums with beautiful red petals that had already blossomed. [When] I took the number 4 bus up Fifth Avenue (it went both uptown and downtown in those days—anyway it's a pretty long trip up to the hospital), it was crowded and I had to stand the whole way getting jostled and squashed, and the flower petals started falling off. [By the time I got to the hospital and] handed Mr. Porter the plant, it only had half its flowers. But he was very gracious and said, "My, what a lovely plant!"

MIKE PEARMAN: I visited Cole at [the hospital] where he had gone for his thirty-second operation. . . . He was greeted by three nurses who said, "Welcome back Mr. Porter. We always enjoy your visits here. You have such interesting guests."

The final script for *Kiss Me, Kate,* as written by Bella Spewack and husband Sam, revolved around Fred Graham, the leading man and director of a second-rate acting company in Baltimore, and his ex-wife, Lilli Venessi, the female lead in the company. Also connected with the company are the romantic interests of Lois Lane and Bill Calhoun, whose plans to marry are continually being thwarted by their bickering over his compulsive gambling. The two couples finally come to terms with themselves while performing *The Taming of the Shrew*.

PATRICIA MORISON: You are quite correct in saying that Cole Porter personally selected me to play the role of Lilli/Kate in *Kiss Me, Kate*. Up to that time I had been primarily an actress under contract to Paramount and was feeling increasingly typecast.

My manager, the late Wynn Rocamora, arranged for me to go with my accompanist to Cole's house on Rockingham to audition for an upcoming show of his. I intentionally prepared all Rodgers and Hammerstein songs, so as not to embarrass Cole. Despite my own apprehension, Cole seemed taken with my singing and asked me to take home the music so that I could study it.

Cole and his associates had the most difficult time raising money for *Kate*. He entertained night after night at his home, playing the score himself and with young performers singing for prospective backers. In the meantime, I signed for one of the first television series and then was booked into Madison Square Garden in New York for a salute to the USO, hosted by Bob Hope.

A year later, Cole called and said that he and his associates had gotten the money for *Kiss Me, Kate* and indicated that I was still his first and only choice for the role of Lilli/Kate. While I was in New York for the USO benefit, and at Cole's request, I auditioned for Jack Wilson and Bella and Sam Spewack. Initially they did not want me, but once I sang, they all concurred with Cole's appraisal of my ability to carry off the demanding role.

During rehearsal and on into the tryout in Philadelphia, the director, producers and most of the cast members tried to convince me to drop the song "I Hate Men," but Cole insisted I keep the number. All the others felt that the song would make me look bad. It was then that I went to Cole and he said, "Just bang the table," and in Philadelphia and again in New York, that number stopped the show. He never doubted for one moment that I could do justice to that song of his.

Early during the New York run, Cole came backstage and told me that his mother had been in the audience that evening and had enjoyed my performance. I jokingly told him I was disappointed in not being able to meet his mother. He returned the next night with his mother in tow. She was delightful and so much like her famous son. A small woman, with dark eyes and very petite features.

When I was doing *The King and I* with Yul Brynner in Los Angeles, Cole came one evening. When I expressed disappointment to someone that he did not come backstage, the next night a massive bouquet of flowers arrived in my dressing room with a wonderfully warm note from Cole. He was such a private person, not easy to know, but once you got to know him he was so kind and so generous, especially in giving encouragement to those he knew had talent.

I met Linda at the Philadelphia opening. She should not have come. She was not at all well and that night she caught pneumonia, which further aggravated her already precarious condition. Linda had great charm and was the personification of class, and still retained vestiges of her once-great beauty. Cole once told me that Linda had taken all her jewels back to Cartier to be sold because she reasoned that her hands were no longer pretty.

I owe so much to my voice teacher, Richard Borchert. He had such great faith in me and worked with me in preparing for the role in *Kiss Me, Kate*. Without his encouragement I could not have met the challenge of that demanding role, for I had not sung in so long prior to being offered the part.

ALEX STEINERT: He never had to fight anyone. He won his battles without fighting. He knew the Spewacks had someone else in mind, but he didn't want to antagonize them. So he sent Pat [Patricia Morison] to New York for a benefit and to visit the Spewacks and they fell in love with her.

COLE PORTER: If she can sing, our problems are solved. We'll create a great new star.

With the exception of Alfred Drake, Cole and the Spewacks went with unknowns. In addition to Patricia Morison, the other roles in *Kate* were filled by Lisa Kirk, Harold Lang, Harry Clark, and Jack Diamond.

COLE PORTER: My show is very exciting! I've written fifteen songs and have five more to do. You'll like the score. It's so simple, as if it had been written by an idiot child.

HELEN HAYES: I regret not owning the Koh-i-noor diamond so that I could tuck it in a nosegay as an appreciation for the joy you've given me with *Kiss Me, Kate*. Bless you, you ever-bloomin' genius.

MARTHA GROVES: Shortly after Cole Porter's *Kiss Me, Kate* opened triumphantly on Broadway in 1948, a friend who had just heard "Some Enchanted Evening" from *South Pacific* asked Porter who had written the song.

"Rodgers and Hammerstein," he replied, "if you can imagine it taking two men to write one song."

Porter, of course, single-handedly wrote hundreds of contagious melodies and witty lyrics. He was the cleverest and most sophisticated popular songwriter of his time. He was a language magician who wrested songwriting from its moon-June-croon rut.

He was also a world traveler, friend of royalty, millionaire and snob. Even Greta Garbo described him as "always so unfriendly."

MIKE CORDA: Cole Porter's music is as vivid today as it was the day it was first heard on Broadway or in the movies, due in large measure to the man's wit and intelligence. It was so marvelously melodic, with great harmonic depth, not at all shallow.

Kate became a hit because it was a rather clever and more arty effort, with a good book and a brilliant Porter score. It was so much better than anything then being offered on Broadway.

It was a sheer joy for me to play, "So In Love," and "Were Thine That Special Face." Even after 1,077 performances on Broadway the music totally captivated me and continues to do so today. The entire score is a monument to Cole's genius and his place in the theatre.

As a 28-year-old musician, the opportunity to be exposed to Cole Porter and his music was a dream come true. I grew up playing and listening on the radio to the Big Bands playing his songs, never realizing that one day I would be involved in a Cole Porter show. I just could not see myself in a theatre playing his music each night; it was a real labor of love for me.

I did not know him personally, but he was not a remote figure—he was very much there during each rehearsal at the Nola Studios. Always fastidiously dressed, never without a red carnation in his buttonhole and never without his cane. Impeccable! He never intruded during rehearsal. If he had something to say, he related it to his fair-haired boy, musical director Pembroke Davenport. In fact, Pembroke is the one who hired me. It was my playing a combination of jazz-symphonic that turned the trick for me.

We all know that Cole hesitated when first approached to do *Kate* by Bella Spewack (co-author of the book with her husband, Sam). The musical, loosely based on Shakespeare's *The Taming of the Shrew*, at first intimidated Cole. Not having had a hit in years, he may have misconstrued his ability to turn a work of the Bard into a successful musical. The fact that he did only brought greater luster to his already recognized genius as a composer.

I myself, and all the others connected with the show, tried just a little bit harder when we knew he was in the audience. It was our way of saluting his genius and a way of showing our thanks for giving us such a big hit.

Among my all-time favorite Cole Porter tunes and ones that I never tire of playing are "Easy to Love," such a tender ballad; "Let's Do It," clever, witty and such musical fun; "Ev'ry Time We Say Goodbye," just enough of a torch tune to bring a tear or two to one's eye; and "So In Love," a great piece of music. We played this one as a reprise in the second act and as an exit march for the audience. Thus the audience left the theatre humming this lovely tune and remembering its creator.

THE PRODUCER OF *Kiss Me, Kate,* John C. "Jack" Wilson, was Cole's friend from those early carefree days in Venice. When each of them returned to New York, the two friends would occasionally run up to Harlem together to partake of the pleasures being offered above 125th Street. Wilson, a near-contemporary of Cole's, became in his mid-twenties the constant companion of Noel Coward. As the lover-manager-business partner of the brilliant Coward, the handsome, debonair Yaleman was also his closest friend in the prewar years. At the outbreak of World War II, Jack Wilson settled permanently in the United States, and he and Coward began to lead increasingly separate lives.

Cole and Jack had a number of things in common. Both were Yalemen, both loved the theater, both were urbane, cultivated, both occasionally drank and smoked to excess, and both were practicing homosexuals married to beautiful, worldly women. Wilson's wife, Natasha "Natalie" Paley, was born to the Imperial Purple—a Russian Romanov princess, daughter of Grand Duke Paul and the granddaughter of Emperor Alexander II. Princess Paley was an exotic beauty who had been considered as a possible bride for Britain's Prince Albert (the Duke of York, later King George VI). However, she chose to marry couturier Lucien Lelong, then divorce him to marry Jack Wilson in 1933.

Natalie Paley Wilson, whose lesbian tendencies were well known, saw excessive drinking and pill-taking turn her great beauty into just a memory. Noel Coward, who adored Natalie, was constantly after her to curb her intake of both alcohol and drugs but the imperious princess would not mend her ways.

Linda and Natalie had great affection for each other, so much so that a portrait of Natalie Wilson by Russian-American painter Pavel Tchelitchew hung in the Porters' Waldorf Towers apartment.

Once Cole Porter was committed to *Kiss Me, Kate,* Porter's great score impressed everyone connected with the production. *Kate* was not just a one- or two-hit show. The music was memorable from beginning to end and its lyrics never flagged, from "Why Can't You Behave?" to "Always True to You in My Fashion" to "Wunderbar." His seventeen numbers for *Kate* revealed his genius.

Despite that genius, financial backers for the show could not be found, and the producers could neither raise money nor interest a big-name star for the show. Jack Wilson wanted Lily Pons for the role of Kate, but Miss Pons felt her health would not permit a rigorous Broadway run. Mary Martin had several talks with Cole, but somehow one of those inexplicable misunderstandings occurred. Miss Martin later confided in Bella Spewack that when she asked to take the music home to study it, Cole replied that it was impossible since his were the only copies. Martin interpreted this to mean he didn't really want her. Meanwhile, Wilson selected a young Hollywood starlet, Patricia Morison, whose own agent doubted that she had the flamboyance to carry the role of Kate. But Cole was captivated by her manner and after she auditioned for the Spewacks she got the part. From the very beginning, Alfred Drake had been marked for the Fred Valenti/Petruchio role. Most of Cole Porter's associates and friends wanted Ann Miller for the Lois/Bianca role, but Cole went to bat wildly for the exuberant Lisa Kirk, and she won the role.

Despite the numerous disagreements over casting, positive feelings about the show ran high from the start. The opening in Philadelphia occurred on December 2, 1948, and although fighting for breath, Linda had managed to proudly take her place beside her husband for this special evening. When the curtain went up on opening night, the creative talents of Porter, the Spewacks and all the other participants came together to produce Cole Porter's masterpiece of the American musical theater. One member of the audience that night, Milton Berle, telephoned New York afterward to say that this show was Cole's greatest hit; the majority of the audience felt the same way.

COLE PORTER: To a person who has talent and is willing to work hard, Broadway in New York is as friendly as Main Street in Peru, Indiana.

The New York Times: Cole Porter has written his best score in years, together with witty lyrics. . . .

The New Yorker: Any man who will rhyme "Cressida" with "Ambassador" is capable of practically anything. . . .

Another honor came Cole's way with the arrival of *Kiss Me, Kate* on Broadway—*Time* magazine had him on the cover of their January 31, 1949, edition.

PATRICE MUNSEL: I loved doing *Kate* [in a road company]. I feel that Kate was the first women's libber and I adored the way she stood up for her rights and at the same time managed to remain a totally attractive female in the process. I always felt that "Too Darn Hot" was the best number in the show and I wasted hours brooding about how to get that song for myself.

Cole Porter once told me he would love to do a musical just for me. Alas, just after he made that statement he became too ill to follow through.

WHEN THE PORTERS arrived back in New York from the December 2 opening, Linda suddenly developed severe lung congestion. She was so desperately ill that she had almost died the night of December 7, 1948. Her doctors decided that as soon as she was able to travel, she should spend the winter at the J6 Ranch in Arizona. Their ever-faithful friend Howard Sturges went along, helping to keep Linda amused during her period of recuperation in the sun.

COLE PORTER (IN A LETTER TO HIS MOTHER, KATE):
Dearest Ma,

I went to Arizona last weekend and found Linda barely improved. The new drug (Aurreomycin [*sic*]) which they had been giving her gave her such nausea that she had to give it up. The day before yesterday they began giving it to her again, with something to alleviate the nausea, so yesterday she was slightly improved, but the sleeplessness, the coughing and the struggle for breath continue. . . .

The greatest thing about her is that she is so philosophical. Her only remark during my last visit, showing that she wasn't in the least discouraged, was, "Oh, Cole, how I would love to bounce again!"

All My Love,
Cole

COLE CONTINUED TO be busy; he had just completed work on Warner Brothers' *Adam's Rib,* starring Katharine Hepburn, Spencer Tracy, David Wayne, and Judy Holliday. Porter's contribution to this comedy, directed by his friend George Cukor, was the song Wayne sings to Hepburn, "Farewell, Amanda." Cole turned all the profits over to the Damon Runyon Cancer Fund (a favorite charity of columnist Walter Winchell and show business people).

With this small film chore out of the way, Cole turned his full attention to *Out of This World,* a production by Lemuel Ayers and Arnold Saint Subber and starring Charlotte Greenwood, William Eythe, Priscilla Gillette and David Burns.

Despite the fact that backers poured money into the new show expecting another *Kate,* things did not work. This show became a total disappointment and Cole was devastated, seeming to realize from the beginning that the show was in deep trouble.

Agnes de Mille, the original director, was upstaged when the brilliant George Abbott was brought in to "doctor" the show. But even this Broadway veteran could not save a show that some said was doomed from the outset by its highly allegorical sets, which overpowered the story line and music in the production.

From Philadelphia the show lumbered on to Boston and eventually opened at the New Century Theatre on December 21, 1950; it closed after only 157 performances.

COLE PORTER: The book was bad. The scenery was so spectacularly great that the audience looked at it and neither heard nor saw the performers.

174

From this disaster, I went on to supervise the Hollywood version of *Kiss Me, Kate,* and added to it a song dropped from *Out of This world* called "From This Moment On." It has since become a standard.

GEORGE ABBOTT: I worked only once with Cole Porter. I was called in to doctor the 1950 production *Out of This World,* taking over for the original director, Agnes de Mille. I went to Boston along with F. Hugh Herbert to try and salvage a show with a good book and some wonderful dance numbers. Yes, I take responsibility for dropping Cole Porter's "From This Moment On" in order to tighten the show.

The New Yorker: *Out of This World* is a remarkably handsome show that contains several of Cole Porter's most typical musical efforts; quite a few excellent performances especially by Charlotte Greenwood and David Burns; and a great deal of the sort of humor that has been diverting Miss Elsa Maxwell for years and apparently still does.

Other critics were less kind, and in order to escape the humiliation visited upon him by the failure of *Out of This World,* Cole and Linda, both now feeling healthier, accompanied by Howard Sturges, fled to Mexico for rest and recuperation.

With one great hit and one great disaster to his credit in just over two years, the beginning of the 1950s would see a decided change in Cole Porter's behavior. He began to feel that his creative flair was gone. Tense and drawn, he suffered from severe headaches and sleepless nights. All of this caused him to gripe to friends at the slightest provocation, an attitude that was untypical of the man. Added to his moodiness was his belief that he was going broke.

Linda felt that a return to Europe might be the right tonic needed to pull him out of this depressed state. With his valet,

Paul Sylvain, Cole flew to Europe for a planned six-week stay in Paris. Unfortunately, however, the lights of that beloved city had gone out for him, and he returned after only a week.

10

"Come Along with Me"

COLE PORTER'S EMOTIONAL condition was far more serious than Linda had at first estimated, and she finally persuaded her husband to check into Doctors' Hospital in Manhattan. Dr. Moorhead, who had become a patient himself, gave instructions for the care of his most famous patient from his own sickbed.

In an effort to alleviate the deepening depression, Cole underwent a series of electric-shock treatments, and after a month of therapy, he was allowed to leave the hospital and continue to recuperate at home.

Although Cole was eager to return to California, he postponed the trip when columnist-turned-television-host Ed Sullivan proposed a two-hour television special, "Salute to Cole Porter," in February 1952.

The television show proved a turning point for Cole. It gave him something else to focus on besides physical ailments and imaginary money problems.

The "Salute to Cole Porter," as seen on Ed Sullivan's "Toast of the Town" program, featured such luminaries as Metropolitan opera star Mimi Benzell; Lisa Kirk singing, "My Heart

Belongs to Daddy," and Dolores Gray paired with William Gaxton to sing "You're the Top." Monty Woolley was also featured in the show, recalling his longstanding friendship with the great composer.

IN 1952, WHILE working on *Can-Can*, Cole received word that his mother had been stricken with a cerebral hemorrhage. Though Kate was ninety, she had remained in reasonably good health; she had even made plans to spend the early fall in New York. By the time Cole arrived in Peru, Indiana, his mother lay in her bedroom unconscious while her two North American Indian maids sat on the floor outside the door, as if at the entrance of a tomb of the ancients.

There was nothing to do except await the inevitable. Linda's condition would not permit her to make the trip; however, Paul Sylvain and Howard Sturges were there with Cole.

For distraction, Cole sat on the back porch intermittently working on the score for *Can-Can*. Kate finally died without regaining consciousness on the morning of August 3, 1952. After a simple service, she was buried in the family plot at Mt. Hope Cemetery in Peru, next to her late husband. As in life, so it was in death—since Cole was everything to her, Kate left him everything she had, including the family home, Westleigh Farms.

Peru Daily Tribune (an editorial): Peru has lost one of its finest residents in the death of Mrs. Kate Cole Porter. She was highly respected and a lovely lady. Mrs. Porter was at home in two worlds, the Hoosier countryside and the world of international society. It was her good fortune to be linked to two great men and to live in two great eras. Her father was a merchant prince, her son a renowned playright. Her father was of the stuff that produced the Carnegies, Fricks and Vanderbilts of his day. Her son has no peers in the American theatre. . . . T. C. Steele, dean of Hoosier artists, once said, "The greatest art is the art of living." Mrs. Porter was a practitioner of this great art.

<hr/>

JAMES OMAR COLE: Kate Porter was very social. You might say the queen bee of Peru society. She imparted this love of the social world to Cole. She was definitely the catalyst that made him into the genius he was to become in the world of music. Without her guiding hand in those very early years and her constant insistence that he adhere to a prescribed routine of study, he would never have achieved recognition on Broadway and beyond.

Howard Sturges often came to Peru. He was beloved by Cole and absolutely adored by Cole's mother. We still maintain the Howard Sturges bedroom at Westleigh Farms. It remains today just the way it was at the time of Kate's death. It was the last time that Cole came back to Indiana. His mother's presence had been the last link to his hometown.

Immediately following his mother's burial, Cole returned to New York, continuing to work on the score for *Can-Can*.

<hr/>

COLE PORTER (IN RESPONSE TO A FRIEND'S INQUIRY): You asked what I am doing. I continue to give small dinners in my little apartment here at the Waldorf. Last night [December 14, 1952] I had Charlie Chaplin and Harry Crocker (Oona was ill), the Bob Sherwoods, and the Bill Paleys. We had a wonderful time. Chaplin took the stage and went on and on. You would have liked it. Tonight Nicky de Gunzburg and I go to see the Balinese dancers, who opened last night. The papers are full of raves.

By the way, Noel Coward's play [*Quadrille*] for the Lunts is one of the biggest hits of his life. We all believe it will continue for quite a few years. It opened in London to unanimous panning by the London critics. The play, however, is so strong and the Lunts such a delight that most people believe it can survive and do beautifully. I sent you Hedda Hopper's book. It is entertaining.

These comments to a friend show that, despite his own physical condition, the recent death of his beloved mother, and the steady decline in Linda's health Cole showed great enthusiasm for life and living.

It was during this same period that this writer met Cole Porter for the first time. The scene of this initial encounter with America's premier composer was the wonderful Colony restaurant, presided over by Gene Cavallero, Sr. (The Colony was hauteur and Italian-style haute cuisine. From the very beginning it was the grandest restaurant in New York and remained so long after Henri Soule's Le Pavillon began to draw away some of its most favored clients. Years earlier, New York's Mayor Jimmy Walker had such a love affair with the Colony that he changed the direction of traffic from east-west to west-east on Sixty-First Street in the block between Madison and Park; this reversal established a traffic pattern that made the Colony more accessible to the mayor's block-long Rolls-Royce.) I was a guest at a dinner party hosted by Rosie Dolly, one of the legendary Dolly Sisters. Because of this we were accorded the honor of being seated in the front lobby (the bar), where Cavallero seated only his most select dinner patrons.

As we finished dinner, the owner's son, Gene Cavallero, Jr., brought a note to Miss Dolly from an adjoining table. Our hostess informed us that Cole Porter had asked her and her entire party to join him for coffee and after-dinner drinks. She and the composer had known each other for thirty years and saw one another frequently in New York.

The composer was hosting a party of three: Marlene Dietrich, Billy Baldwin, and Natasha Paley Wilson. Cole welcomed us, and he and Rosie introduced their respective guests and then instructed the captain to take drink orders.

As a youth who had grown up with a glamorous, flapper-era mother, I regarded Cole Porter's name and music as part of a certain mystique associated with a time and frame-of-mind that had been with me since my earliest childhood.

I was transfixed by the living embodiment of the legend. And then I was struck by how frail and vulnerable the man appeared—the musical giant who had written all those witty, insouciant lyrics was just a wisp of a man, but one whose personal magnetism outshone his frailty. Even the well-known Dietrich ego was no match for the brilliant mind and conversation of Cole Porter. As for me, being a mere twenty-one years of age, and despite having been exposed early on to a world of highly sophisticated adults, my contribution to that memorable evening was that of a listener.

Another aspect of the man that I was taken with at that first meeting was the high, metallic quality of his voice, with its decided, clipped accent and just a touch of a lisp, especially in a rush of words. Cole Porter's speaking voice was very reminiscent of that of the self-indulgent ex-king, the Duke of Windsor.

The conversation that heady evening ranged over many things: Cole telling Natasha that she should set an example for her husband, Jack, in her efforts to control his drinking habits, which were beginning to ruin his health; Marlene expressing in icy Germanic terms her gratitude for Cole "giving" her "The Laziest Gal in Town," and asking him to write a special song for a new revue she was mounting; Cole and Billy comparing notes and catching up in a gossipy way on all their mutual friends; Rosie Dolly telling Cole that on one of her frequent visits to Venice in the mid-twenties, he had promised to write an entire show for her and her sister, Jennie; she ended her comments by saying that the only thing the Dolly Sisters lacked in their long career was a Cole Porter musical. The evening concluded with Cole expressing how wonderful he felt being back in the harness, readying another Broadway show.

Cole Porter had a precise sense of time. His car had been called for 11 P.M., and before departing at precisely 10:55 P.M. (I was intrigued that it was not 11 P.M. or 10:45 P.M., but exactly five minutes to the hour of eleven), Cole arose, spoke to each of us at the table and asked another member of the Dolly party to bring me up to Williamstown. (The guest, who had a summer home in the Berkshires, had been talking with Cole about the area's tranquility and attractions and mentioned that I often went there on weekends, and I subsequently was privileged to see Cole Porter on two occasions during brief visits to Williamstown. Unfortunately the visits were cut short because of his health.)

The last time I saw Cole was at a party given by mutual friends for Beatrice Lillie during one of Lady Peel's frequent Manhattan sojourns. It was an intimate party, and we reminisced briefly about that night at the Colony. He spoke of how he was looking forward to returning to California to begin work on a new film project. Again I was taken by the man's fragile, yet determined, hold on life and realized as I had at my first encounter with this musical genius that the glue that held him together was work, work, work.

LINDA WAS UNABLE to attend the Broadway premiere of Cole's *Can-Can* at the Shubert Theatre on May 7, 1953. The Feuer-Martin production starred French-import Lilo and the distinguished American actor Peter Cookson. The notices were mixed, with most of the credit going to the dance numbers by Michael Kidd and the exuberant personality of Gwen Verdon. Under the able direction of Abe Burrows, the show racked up 892 performances on Broadway, making it Cole Porter's second-longest running musical.

Despite her absence, just before Cole left for opening night, Linda saw to it that he received his traditional presentation case. Made of fourteen-karat gold and designed by Duc di

Verdura, it had a wavy, reeded pattern with the words *Can-Can* worked into an interlocking monogram. The interior was engraved, "*Can-Can,* New York, May 7, 1953." This was the last cigarette case Linda was to give Cole.

Newsweek: And Cole Porter's nostalgic score—while admittedly not one of his best—changes a surprisingly old-fashioned book with melody and bounce.

The New Yorker: Of the actors I was particularly taken with Gwen Verdon, whose Eve adds at least one extra dimension to that celebrated character and whose performance throughout is one of the delights of the season.

Mr. Porter's tunes are, as always, cheerful and adept, but there are enough echoes from the past to distress those whose memories go back more than a dozen years, and the words too often have what I can describe only as a sort of faded chic.

COLE PORTER: Once again [the critics say] it's not from my top drawer. . . .

ABE BURROWS: He wouldn't change a waltz into a beguine. He didn't like that. He'd look at you calmly and say, "I'll give you another," but he wouldn't change that one. He wouldn't bend a song. Songs get bent and changed and ruined.

LENA HORNE: "It's All Right With Me" became one of my biggest hits and remains in my repertoire to this day. . . .

PEMBROKE DAVENPORT: I think his indifference to any particular style was not deliberate. I think it was purely instinctive. There was never anything deliberate about his harmonies—they just happened.

The music was bad and the songs had no future.

GWEN VERDON: Prior to *Can-Can*, I had been around quite a bit. I did not star in *Can-Can* but it was the first time I had become recognized in magazines like *Dance Magazine* and *Theatre Arts Magazine*. I was known in the dance world but in terms of an audience, that was the first time I had a speaking part and a miniscule singing part. Of course, I had a major dance role. Being a character that was part of the book, not just a dancer who stepped out and did something, was terrific. For me it was a major step.

The critics were not crazy about the show. They loved the choreography of Michael Kidd. But they gave Cole Porter his usual review for some reason, and this was true of all of his shows, which said, "that Cole Porter was not up to his usual standards." But of course out of this show there were five songs that became standards and are played to this day. His lyrics are so literate. Dorothy Fields, Yip Harburg and Cole Porter, I mean the way they do inner rhymes and the intelligence and wit of the people; the poet in them comes out.

Cole Porter's life-style was largely responsible for his music. He was part of The Roaring Twenties. He was from a very wealthy family. He was part of the polo set. Now, I guess they call it the Jet Set. You know, you fly to Paris for dinner.

Can-Can was my first encounter with Cole Porter, I had never before even seen the man. I knew of him but that was the first time I had ever seen him. He would arrive every day at the rehearsal hall on Second Avenue with spats on his shoes. He always wore a rosebud in his lapel, just like Harold Arlen, and he wore a derby. Up to that time I thought derbies were props in the band, I did not think people wore derbies. He always carried a walking stick but I never realized he had an infirmity; his walking stick looked like the rest of his costume, to go along with the spats and the derby. Knowing his background, I thought that was part of the Cole Porter look.

Not knowing this aspect of his life, every time I looked out at him during rehearsal, I noticed he would wince, and with my own insecurity I thought he was giving me a critical look. Well, after a few days I discovered he was in terrible pain. I learned that many nights he was in such pain he would sleep in a suspended harness, where he would be supported much in the way you would incapacitate a horse, where you would get it off its feet. I guess if he could have been put in water so that his own body weight would have been supported by water, it might have eased his pain. Unlike many stories I have read, I never saw him in a hospital bed on stage during a rehearsal. But at the time *Can-Can* began to take shape, I did not even know that he was suffering.

Cole Porter would never allow anyone to write absolutely original dance music for dance numbers, not even a variation on a theme. He would always use Genevieve Pitot and it was always Cole Porter's music, even if it went on for sixteen choruses it was Cole Porter.

The instrumentation of course would be different, but no one even took a song and then evolved that into dance music—it had to be Cole Porter's. To my knowledge he would only allow Genevieve Pitot to do the dance music for his shows; of course, she did *Can-Can* and *Kiss Me, Kate*. It would always be the same chorus of a song by the yards. And when they would orchestrate it, it would sound different because there would be variation in the instrumental—it could be violins, brass and then something else and something else, but it's still Cole Porter by the yard; in that respect it was boring. It was never music written specifically for the dance, with the sound of the period and the flavor of Cole Porter. It was not like musicals, even two years later, when we did *Damn Yankees,* where they would just open up the middle of a song and do all brand new themes. It's a lot more interesting, at least if you're doing it eight times a week for two years.

Linda Porter was very much there, not that she would come to rehearsal, but he always spoke of his wife. For the opening of *Can-Can*, she gave a cigarette case of fourteen-karat gold. . . . I think *Can-Can* was the twenty-first case that she had given him since knowing him. She always gave it to him the night before the opening at one of the previews, so that he could carry it with him on opening night. And it was always inscribed. This particular case said what the critics would say, which was, "Cole Porter was not up to his usual standards." Apparently they said that anytime he wrote any show, from the time he wrote his first shows at Yale way back when. He did those Yale shows and they thought, "Here's a brilliant new man on the scene," and from then on every review said, "Cole Porter is not up to his usual standards."

I did get one handwritten note from Cole when *Damn Yankees* opened, handwritten on beautiful robin's egg blue stationery. The note said, "When did you get that beautiful low voice?" He must have gone right home from the *Damn Yankees* opening and written it. . . . In *Can-Can* I had to sing like a soubrette and it started on A, while A-flat or B was my big note. Normally I [do] have a very low voice.

I do remember a number of songs from *Can-Can*, especially Peter Cookson singing, "It's All Right With Me." He was fabulous! Peter is such a gentleman. And when later it was sung by Frank Sinatra and Tony Bennett and became a big hit harmony-wise, that was such a beautiful song.

Peter Cookson and his wife, Beatrice Straight, had just gotten married prior to the opening of *Can-Can*. Beatrice Straight gave Peter a huge basket of flowers with a note on opening night. He tore open the envelope which contained the note, which was tied to all those beautiful flowers in the basket. He read the note, kept the note and threw away the envelope. Learning later that Beatrice had enclosed diamond cuff links in the envelope, they searched everywhere and hours later found the discarded envelope with the diamond cuff links.

When we left the theater opening night, it was so crazy—hordes of people mobbed Shubert Alley. Police on horseback had to be called to make it possible for us to get into the Astor Hotel. I went upstairs to see Jack Cole. Jack and I had spent all those years together. We had a brief reunion, which was so important to me.

Beatrice and Peter Cookson said come to the house. . . . I think it was on East 62nd Street. I had never before been in a townhouse. I had never even seen a townhouse other than in a photograph. At the entrance you were greeted by a black-and-white marble floor in a diamond pattern. I had never seen one except in a mansion in the movies; I had never walked on one until this glorious night, a night we all owed to Cole Porter and *Can-Can*.

And because on opening night the show had been stopped because of the dance number I did that Michael Kidd choreographed, the press went bananas. They were searching for me everywhere. Peter Cookson and Beatrice Straight hid me out in a little, old den-type office room. I was really afraid to leave their house. The press had gathered outside their . . . townhouse, and the street was totally blocked off to traffic because of reporters and photographers. It was like today's paparazzi, it was insane. I had never been close to anything like that before. I spoke to only one member of the press, Earl Wilson. It was so mind-boggling for me, but Beatrice calmed me down with, "Stay, my dear." It was three o'clock in the morning when the reporters and photographers finally left.

I must not forget another wonderful thing that happened to

me as a result of *Can-Can* that night. Averell Harriman sent me an entire tree of brown orchids. I had never before seen brown orchids, let alone received even a single orchid before.

PETER COOKSON: Even though it's been over thirty years since I was plunged into the hurly-burly of being in a musical on Broadway, *Can-Can* still seems to have been a high point in my career, even surpassing my experience in *The Heiress*. It still haunts me as an almost dreamlike two years for more than one reason. It was a true mixture of pleasure and pain.

I had always enjoyed singing, but only for my own means. But to open up in front of a cast of professionals during rehearsals—which were always a daily audition—nothing had prepared me as a "straight actor" for the fever that is generated in a high-powered musical being put together. The competition was quite fierce.

In the beginning I had several songs that fit and were written for the part, but some of them were acquired by Lilo, "Allez-Vous-En" and "C'est Magnifique" being the ones I really enjoyed singing. But every time I sang them to her I could hear the wheels of her mind going round and round. So when I lost them I began to feel the ground under my feet beginning to shake. Was I being eased out?

One day as I went into the rehearsal hall on Second Avenue, I noticed this magnificent old Rolls-Royce with a liveried driver waiting at the curb. I went into the hall not knowing what to expect. There he was, Cole Porter, sitting in a chair against the wall, black suit, bowler hat, a cane in his hand, his face a mask, as if his mind were somewhere in the past. The air was electric. It was the master come to judge. It wasn't long before I realized there was no absentmindedness on his part, just pure concentration. But still, there was something anachronistic about his presence in that rowdy, almost bawdy run-through. Something almost ghostlike about him. And why not? How much had he seen in life compared to the rest of us? I was not the only one who was intimidated by his self-composure and remoteness. A true Mandarin. When it was over, he spoke a few encouraging words and then left.

I didn't see him again that I remember until the final run-through in Philadelphia. I was having trouble, I was in trouble. When I sang I could feel the tension in the cast, in Abe Burrows, in Cy Feuer and Ernie Martin. Couldn't seem to let go. They all gave me notes that only made me tighter and more nervous. Then once again there was Cole, relaxed and serene. He came up to me, spoke softly: "Don't worry about your voice. Think of the words and what you are saying. Try it once more." I sang again, looking at him. He smiled, nodded, "That's it." And it was.

The day of the dress rehearsal there was a scene change that took longer than anticipated. The change had to be covered by something in front of the curtain, in one, as they say. That evening, opening night, I was given a costume change, music sheets were thrust into my hand. That night I sang the [new] song for the first time, with the conductor, Milton Rosenstock, mouthing the words in the pit. It went over very well. It was "It's All Right With Me." As far as I know, Cole had written it a few hours earlier and had the confidence in me to sing it almost cold. From then on there was no more fear or pain. I belonged!

I don't think I ever saw Cole Porter again to speak to. But I'll always remember him, for giving me confidence, that thin crippled little man, in his black suit, black tie, bowler hat and cane, his pale face, his eyes filled with memories of pain and pleasure, still able to write so well of love, knowing that soon it would all be over, but caring until the end—the end of an era.

Lilo gave a superb performance at opening night. Once the reviews were in and Gwen Verdon won raves from the critics, things changed. Lilo would step onto the stage and when she went to open her mouth, her throat tightened up and her voice was never the same.

ELSA MAXWELL: He was still badly crippled and facing more surgery when Linda fell ill from gradual thickening in her lungs.... Cole knew there was no hope. He spent much time in her Waldorf Towers apartment, across the hall from his. He would sing his new songs to her and her eyes would brighten. It was because he worked late at night (in the beginning of his career but not at this point in his life) and didn't want Linda disturbed that he maintained separate quarters. Toward the cruel end I believe Linda knew. But true to the Cole Porter legend, she never let him know she knew. That was May 1954.

Linda Lee Porter died on May 20, 1954; she was not quite 71. Linda had hoped to leave Cole an even two million when she died. However, it was not to be; her gross estate, all left to Cole, was assessed at $1,939, 671, possibly underassessed for tax purposes.

Peru Tribune: Cole Porter left bulk of wife's estate.

MRS. IRVING BERLIN (LETTER TO COLE):

Dear Cole:

I found the telegram waiting last night—called Irving in California. We talked a long time about our lovely Linda. He asked me to write you for him as well as me to say how sad we are—and how we remember and always will remember her beauty—not only her face and voice, but everything that was Linda. And I speak of my abiding gratitude for her understanding and imaginative kindness to me when I was a not very happy child.

Devotedly,

Ellin

Letters, notes and telegrams poured in offering Cole words of sympathy and encouragement, and none was more poignant than the letter from Porter's longtime surgeon, Dr. John Moorhead:

Dear Cole:

Telegram just received giving the sad news. Our sympathy goes out to you, and no one more than myself knows how hard the going will be for you. My memory takes me back to the long days of anxiety you gave her when you were hurt—how much she did to sustain you—and may I tell you again she was a pillar of strength to me also at times. Then it was your turn to understandingly and everlastingly bring strength and hope to her—and she knew, how much she rejoiced in it! A rare person of infinite charm and understanding was Linda; and her belief and faith in you never failed even though fighting to get her breath.

Let me be of any help if you need me.

Very sincerely,

M.

JAMES OMAR COLE: Here is Linda's headstone [at the family plot in Peru's Mount Hope Cemetery]. Linda had wanted to be buried at Buxton Hill at Williamstown, but Cole made this decision to bring her "home" to Indiana.

I was never close to Linda. Knew her only casually. Never met her more than three times in my life. Most times she did not come to Westleigh Farms, when Cole made his annual pilgrimage at Christmastime. It was always understood that her health prevented her from making those trips. Those

191

Christmas holidays were wonderful. Kate and Cole entertained at a big family dinner right here in the family dining room. It was so festive and Cole not only played traditional Christmas music but many of his own songs. Kate was so proud!

ELSA MAXWELL: In the intervening years, Cole often must have been lonely. But of this he has given no sign. He continued to delight his friends with his wit and charm and to enchant his public with his gay melodic songs.

As a final tribute to Linda's great beauty and to the contribution she had made to his life, Cole, on August 28, 1954, was granted a patent on the "Linda Porter rose." The strain was developed from the crossing of two varieties of tea roses, the "Senator Potie" and the "Ponsettia." The blossom is pink and unusually fragrant. This tribute insured, at least among rose fanciers, that Linda would be remembered for something other than just being the wife of a famous composer.

COLE CONTINUED TO work at breakneck speed on *Silk Stockings,* the new Feuer and Martin *(Can-Can)* production, with a book by George S. Kaufman, Leueen McGrath, and Abe Burrows. The plot of *Silk Stockings* closely resembled the MGM film *Ninotchka* that was made famous by the presence of Greta Garbo. German-import Hildegarde Neff would portray the role of the Russian commissar who falls in love with Paris and all that the city has to offer. Assisting in the cast were Don Ameche, Gretchen Wyler, and Julie Newmar.

Cole flew to Detroit to add the final touches to the *Silk Stockings* score prior to its New York opening. However, instead of his usual optimism regarding his latest Broadway-bound play, he pleaded prior commitments in Europe and set off for Switzerland for a three-and-a-half month journey on the continent.

Silk Stockings opened at the Imperial Theatre on February 24, 1955, after an arduous out-of-town tryout, during which authors changed, the original choreographer was dropped, and changes were made on top of changes in the story line. The only constant in the show was Cole Porter's Broadway score, which would be his last.

The New Yorker: The tunes, perhaps, are not in Mr. Porter's topmost vein, but they are spirited and appropriate, and the lyrics, containing, if Miss Maxwell will forgive me, the usual quota of special, upper-middle-class references, still have a style that no one else can command.

Silk Stockings cost $370,000 to mount—in those days an all-time high for a Broadway musical. Cole Porter's score for the show must be credited for its run of 478 performances, which enabled the producers to recover the enormous production expenses.

MEANWHILE, COLE WAS being entertained like a visiting nabob on every stop of his longest European journey in years. In Monte Carlo he was honored at a dinner party hosted by Prince de Polignac and Princess Charlotte of Monaco, the parents of Prince Ranier. He had a brief reunion with Sir Charles Mendl, the husband of the late Elsie de Wolfe. The titled aristocracy of Italy vied with each other for his attention, and shipping magnate Stavros Niarchos loaned him his beautiful ebony yacht, *Eros,* for a two-week cruise of the Greek Islands. Cole loved all the attention and was in high spirits during this European sojourn.

Cole returned to New York on June 7, 1955, and immediately took up residence in his newly decorated apartment on the thirty-third floor at the Waldorf Towers; his tranquil, nine-room retreat had just been finished by decorator Billy Baldwin.

In *Billy Baldwin Remembers*, the decorator describes his work on Cole's apartment:

> Cole Porter was abroad when I completed my work on his apartment in the Waldorf Towers (Truman Capote was later to write that I had "transformed it into an island of sublime and subtle luxury"). When Cole stepped through the door of Apartment 33A for the first time, he just looked around in amazement.
>
> "Is this all mine?" he said.
>
> It all was. He had inherited everything from his wife, Linda, who had lovingly collected every bit of the beautiful French furniture in Paris before the war. Cole had lived with it for years, scarcely aware of it. Now that it all belonged to him, he felt a responsibility. "In order to really possess your possessions," he said to me, "you must know and understand them."
>
> Right after he moved in, he pasted up two charts side by side on his shaving mirror: one of English kings, one of French kings, both dating from the 17th Century. That was the start of his education. He learned quickly, and grew very knowledgeable about his treasures. He was proud of them not as status symbols, but for the very fine things they were.

Vogue: While Cole was in Europe, work progressed on the remodeling and decorating of Apartment 33-A in the Waldorf Towers. Billy Baldwin created a masterpiece in decorating and design. The filtered glow of an English country house—clear, keyed-up colors and day-long floods of sun gave this great-roomed city apartment a quality of detachment from city life. ... The most ingenious room in the newly-designed apartment was the tortoise-walled library; three walls were banked with free-standing bookcases put together out of shimmery brass piping, which sets up a fleeting thrust and parry of light rays. These book units gave Cole's library in the nine-room Towers apartment a cachet that decorators have been trying to emulate ever since.... From Cole's house in Paris came two painted and tasseled Regence canapes and a magnificent Louis XV sofa placed against the right wall. At the far end of this room, two pianos stood back-to-back; on the keyboard of one, a mug of pencils for editing scores, and Cole's spectacles and the ever-present caramels from Arnold's Candies in Peru, Indiana.

The entire apartment was a tribute to the design genius of Billy Baldwin and a living monument to the woman who inspired it—Linda Lee Porter—who, prior to her death had gone over every detail of the design with Baldwin, thus assuring Cole the comfort so necessary to his well-being and a constant reminder of the irreplaceable helpmate who had been the most supportive person of his life.

SHORTLY AFTER HIS return from Europe, word reached Cole that Howard Sturges had died in Paris. The death of his longtime friend from the Paris days of the twenties seemed to take a far heavier toll on Cole than the death of his mother or Linda. Sturges, the Rhode Island aristocrat, had been part of the triumvirate (with Kate and Linda) that had kept Cole going, and had rekindled the flame when it was going out. He had sustained Cole both in his personal and professional life. Howard Sturges was always there and now he, too, was gone.

BENJAMIN STURGES: While [Howard] had a number of close friends in Paris, New York and Hollywood, there was never any question but that the people closest to him outside the family were the Porters, and that he was devoted to them both.

He had a wonderful and delightfully irreverent sense of humor and even though he denied it, I can't help thinking that some of the lyrics in Cole's songs derived from Howard.

This was an interesting thought from the nephew of Howard Sturges. Could it have been that Howard Sturges played the role of the Earl of Southampton to Cole Porter's Shakespeare? It must be noted that Cole Porter never wrote another Broadway musical after Howard Sturges's death.

Cole's immediate reaction to the death of his great friend was one of enormous sadness. Then, when he realized that he was alone and that his life would also soon be over, it seemed to mark the beginning of the end in a life that, in spite of its touch of tragedy, had been so full.

11

"Good-bye, Little Dream, Good-bye"

THE SUDDEN LOSS of Howard Sturges continued to gnaw at Cole Porter; its effect on him would show itself in both his spirit and the quality and quantity of his work during the time that remained. It would be cumulative and ultimately it would serve to stifle forever one of the great talents in the American theater, for Howard Sturges was far more than a friend to Cole Porter. He was, in fact, his alter ego.

Despite the emotional and physical pain, Cole continued to attend to his daily routine very much as he had always done. Every morning in New York he was up about 9:30 or 10, had a massage (given by the man the rest of the staff hated, suspecting that his duties went beyond those of just providing Cole with the medically prescribed massages), and exercised. Then his barber and he would also have sunlamp treatments. At lunchtime, he was joined by his faithful secretary, Madeline Smith. He ate very little, using the time to dispose of his still-voluminous mail and to attend to minor business matters.

Occasionally, his health permitting, he would take lunch out, with one or two friends, at Le Pavillon (which Cole facetiously called his "little boarding house, simple but good") or the Colony.

In the evenings a few close friends were often asked for dinner. Those small dinner parties were always elegant and served with great precision. The table was always attractive and the food good and beautifully served by waiters from the Waldorf-Astoria Hotel.

The host always wore a Malmaison carnation* in his button-hole. The repartée between the host and his guests was reputed to be quite brilliant.

On weekends, Cole traveled in his chauffeur-driven car to Buxton Hills in Williamstown; great effort was always made by Mrs. Smith to see to it that one or two guests were asked up to Cole's country retreat, so as to lessen the boredom that increased after Linda's death.

Cole continued his breakneck work schedule, turning out the score for the MGM film *High Society*, starring Grace Kelly, Bing Crosby, Frank Sinatra, Celeste Holm, Louis Armstrong, and Louis Calhern, and featuring the hit song "True Love."

In early June 1956, two more films for MGM occupied Cole's time, *Silk Stockings* and *Les Girls*. Completing these last two films in less than enthusiastic fashion, he entered the hospital in New York, where he was operated on for a large, inflamed gastric ulcer on January 8, 1957. Following the surgery, he recuperated at the Montego Bay estate of the William Paleys. Returning to New York, Cole was elated to learn that "True Love" was up for an Academy Award. For the first time in his life he hired a press agent to assist in promoting the tune, which had the high-priced talents of Bing Crosby and Grace Kelly both in the film and as a duet on the fast-selling record-ing. However, in typical Porter fashion he refused to personally promote either the music or himself.

Again, Cole was not to be honored by his peers—his lovely song lost out to "Que Sera, Sera," a song from a Hitchcock

*The Malmaison carnation is a variety named in honor of the home of the Empress Josephine of France, where it was first developed.

movie. Some felt that he had lost out because he was regarded by Hollywood as a "highbrow" songwriter. However, it was no secret in show business that Cole had always found Bing Crosby lacking when it came to performing his works, and he laid much of the blame on Bing Crosby's interpretation of "True Love."

April 1957 found Cole in Italy, touring the peninsula for a month, returning to some of his haunts in Venice. In the heyday of Cole, Noel, Elsa, and Linda and their court of preening peacocks, it had seemed like the last bastion of every imperial dynasty. Cole Porter sat alone on the Grand Canal with the cane that was no longer an affectation, as it had been in his earlier days in both Paris and Venice. The cane was now an absolute necessity.

The smart sartorial splendor that he sported in his heyday had given way to dark suits for daywear and dinner clothes for more formal occasions. Gone were the plaids and checks and the vivid shirts that had marked his years at Yale and in the society world. Never the fashion pacesetter that his friend the Duke of Windsor was, Cole was nonetheless always capable of making a fashion statement. Now, it was only in Hollywood that he allowed himself to be less formal in his dress; in the movie colony he affected casual trousers in bright hues and colorful shirts, frequently in Hawaiian prints.

Cole made efforts to see friends during this trip, and during a stopover in Rome he visited Bricktop's night club, but was unsuccessful in meeting up with his pal from the Paris of the twenties.

BRICKTOP: I missed a chance for a reunion with an old friend because of my chronic tardiness, and I will regret it until the end of my days. Cole Porter came to Rome. He was staying at the Grand Hotel and sent word around that he would be coming to Bricktop's. I wrote him a note saying I would be at the club at ten-thirty on the night he wanted to come. I knew from experience that if you told Cole Porter ten-thirty you had better be there at ten-thirty. I was five minutes late. As I arrived by cab and was entering the club, I saw a car drive away. Angelo (my club manager) told me that a woman had come downstairs looking for me, and I just knew I had missed Cole. I wrote him a note telling him how sorry I was. He wrote back, "The sign read Bricktop's, but I didn't see any Brick."

When I returned permanently to New York, I frequently telephoned Cole but he would never accept any of my calls.

DOUGLAS FAIRBANKS, JR.:   Cole had class in everything he did—it was such a part of both his public and private image. His life-style, the house in Paris, the palazzo in Venice, the lavish apartment at the Waldorf Towers, the Brentwood estate on the West Coast, and the country retreat in Williamstown. He was first class!

Cole's music certainly reflected the times in which he lived and worked. He had a view of the world from the top—from the very highest level of society. Top drawer! It was a world of millionaire Americans and their titled counterparts in Europe, with a sprinkling of theatrical personalities. The same world inhabited by and written about by Noel Coward.

I remember well, one of the last times I saw Cole, he told me how the idea for "Night and Day" first came to him during the time he was on a flatboat going down the Rhine in the late 1920s. The idea for the song sprung to life while he was getting over a hangover after a night of too much German beer.

ALEX STEINERT: He knew good writing. He knew when to double a chord, he knew when not to double a chord. He was aware of voice leading, which is the secret of a great many of his things. And above all he had taste.

ROBERT MONTGOMERY: Cole never was a businessman, he wasn't interested in it and rejected any kind of notion of a producing role. It wasn't until 1949 or '48 that John Wharton persuaded Cole that he should have an interest in the pockets of his publishers. Cole really had to be brought, dragging and screaming, to the idea that he would even have an interest in his own publishing, whereas Rodgers and Hammerstein, they formed their own publishing company.

DUCHESS OF ALBA: Cole was very kind to my father, always bringing or sending him many beautiful objects and mementos as a reminder of their long and enduring friendship. [These objects are now scattered throughout the many palaces in Spain that the Duchess calls home.]

COLE WORKED THE entire summer and fall of 1957 on the score of what would be his only television musical, an adaptation of the story of Aladdin by the *New Yorker* humorist, S. J. Perelman. The score reflected Cole's meticulous attention to detail, but unfortunately there was little else—and no great tunes—to commend it, or for that matter the production itself.

Even a cast of such stellar names as Cyril Ritchard, Basil Rathbone, Una Merkel, and Dennis King could not light up *Aladdin*. It was produced by Richard Lewine and shown on CBS-TV on February 21, 1958, as part of Du Pont's "Show of the Month" series, and it turned out to be a $500,000 flop. Cole never wrote anything else after *Aladdin*. It is indeed ironic that the man who had been one of our most original and distinctive composers, contributing so much to musical theater, should end his career on a sour note in a totally new medium.

RICHARD LEWINE: The program was at the end of Porter's active life. He went into the hospital before the broadcast and though

I was to see him a few times after the show, he became more and more of a recluse.

There is a great deal of misinformation abroad about "Aladdin" and it keeps being perpetuated in biographies and "fact books." For instance the song "Wouldn't It Be Fun," the last song he wrote, was never in the show although it is in the cast album, which had been recorded two weeks before the broadcast.

S. J. Perelman wrote the book of the show, and he and I went to the coast in 1957, nine months before the program date, to spend several days with Cole discussing song ideas, casting, and the general approach. Any reference in other "bios" to Porter not having the songs ready—or to rewriting—or any problems at all with the score are pure invention. He was prompt, kept every promise and was a delight to work with.

Ralph Nelson, who directed the show, didn't join us until just before rehearsals so it was I who kept in close touch with Cole about song ideas and casting. Irene Sharaff did the costumes, Russell Bennett the orchestrations, Robert Dolan conducted, etc. It was quite a distinguished group.

You state that the show "was not a critical success." It was not a critical success with *New York Times* critic Jack Gould, who already had an unmatched record for panning programs that the other critics—and the audience—liked. There were glowing articles about it afterward—more evidence of perpetuated misinformation. The cast album was very successful and was re-issued twice after the program.

Finally, it must be remembered that this was 90 minutes of extremely difficult, complicated *live* television: a cast of 60, including an elephant, orchestra of 35, technical crew of about 50, etc., etc., with no film, tape or retakes.

On January 14, 1958, approximately a month before *Aladdin's* showing, Cole was admitted to Columbia-Presbyterian Hospital. When told that his right leg would have to be amputated, Cole faced the situation with his usual Spartan stoicism. The night before the operation, he informed his valet, Paul, and his chauffeur, Andrew Bentley. "When Mr. Porter told me about the surgery, I choked up," Bentley reported, "But he was the calmest man in the hospital."

When Cole had healed sufficiently, he was fitted with an artificial leg. Although he was eventually able to walk, Cole told anyone who would listen that, no matter the pain, he would rather have kept his own leg. Time and again, he bemoaned, "I'm only half a man now."

Another blow struck in July 1959 when his faithful valet and friend Paul Sylvain died of cancer. Cole's despondency, combined with a lack of interest in food and his persistent overindulgence in drinking and smoking, had a decidedly deleterious effect on his health.

NOEL COWARD: The time in New York, as usual, was fairly hectic. I visited Cole Porter twice in the hospital. He has at last had his leg amputated and the lines of ceaseless pain have been wiped from his face. He is a bit fretful about having to manage his new leg, but he will get over that. I think if I had to endure all those years of agony I would have had the damned thing off at the beginning, but it is a cruel decision to have to make and it involves much sex, vanity and many fears of being repellent. However, it is now done at last, and I am convinced that his whole life will cheer up and that his work will profit accordingly.

ROBERT MONTGOMERY: He has every intention of getting to work, but he is not ready yet to concentrate.

Because he had no confidence in the artificial leg, Cole refused to go out to dine with friends in their homes, thus giving rise to rumors that he had become a recluse. While it was true that he seldom went out, he always had one or more guests every night for dinner. Among his guests were Ethel Merman, Louise Bearss, Abe Burrows, Mrs. Sumner Wells, Leonard Bernstein, Baron de Gunzburg, Garson Kanin and Ruth Gordon, and Mrs. William Woodward (whose family became the subject of lurid headlines and, recently, a novel after her son had been killed by Mrs. Woodward's daughter-in-law). It always fell to Madeline Smith to see that one or more of these friends were called on a regular basis and invited to dinner at Cole's apartment.

MADELINE P. SMITH: For twenty years he walked with a cane after the initial bout with wheelchair and crutches, and it was not until 1958 that the right leg was finally amputated to save his life. Try as he might he could never overcome this tragedy. He became withdrawn to the point where doctors advised him to always have someone with him. So his lunch was always eaten beside my desk—and often much of it thrown away by me at his direction so his valet would think that he had eaten most of it.

We tried to cheer him all we could, and invited one or two persons to dinner every night: Mrs. William Woodward, Anita Loos, George Eells, Baron de Gunzburg. Mrs. William Randolph Hearst and her sister, Anita Irwin, were faithfuls whom he always enjoyed although at this stage of his life it was not easy to keep up a sustained conversation. He preferred to let others carry the load, and sometimes he fell asleep while guests were there.

Through his many hospitalizations I never heard a word of complaint. Once when I visited him in the hospital, bringing him his mail and magazines, he said his head was cold. So I bought him a cream-colored soft cap with a peak to wear to bed. He tipped it to his nurses in polite good-mornings and wore it all the time. Sometimes I read to him, though he tired easily. He particularly liked *Acu, Acu,* but we never found out where those monstrous look-alike stone statues on Easter Island were from. I wonder if we will ever know?

His latter years found him much more remote from his fellow citizens, for his health had begun to fail him more than ever. It was in 1937 that he had the dreadful accident at the Piping Rock Club on Long Island. . . . It was only the skill and care of the great Dr. John Moorhead, who fought ceaselessly—and always with Mrs. Porter's cooperation—that his legs were preserved from amputation for so many years.

ROBERT MONTGOMERY: In the early '50s, he moved around quite easily, then he had the amputation . . . and it was after that that he really became more homebound, but also much more depressed, he really went into a deep depression then. In a way, today, I wonder if anything could have been done for him—I have no medical knowledge, but I wonder. He certainly had the best medical care possible, and I'm sure that the doctors knew, both from Linda and from everybody else, how serious this would be. I used to see him in the early '50s when he was in New York and he was a joyful, pleasant person to be with. It was always fun to have lunch with Cole because he was full of stories and full of life and in the '60s it was such a trial. He was deeply depressed and we'd go and have lunch . . . and sometimes he would just withdraw so thoroughly that I remember luncheons where I would go and make conversation the entire luncheon—and that's very hard to do when you don't have anyone responding to you.

TED FETTER: The last time I ever had any contact with Cole was because of Monty [Woolley]. I was in television for the latter part of my acting career and I was in the commissary at Twentieth Century-Fox having lunch when Monty, who I hadn't seen in a very long time, and barely recognized except you had to recognize him—even though he'd become a rather old and decrepit man with a kind of yellowing beard—came pattering over to where I was sitting and said, "You've got to go over and see Cole." I was surprised because I was under the impression he and Cole were not that close in the end of their lives. I don't think they really had a quarrel, they may have for all I know, but their relationship was not nearly as close in the latter years of Cole's life. But anyway, Monty came and said, "You've got to see Cole. He's not well at all and he's out at his house in Westwood and he won't see you if you call him up in advance, so go see him but go before five o'clock in the afternoon. Just ring the bell and say you're there," and I said I would try to do it.

Well I didn't get there until about five-thirty and the nurse came to the door; a lady in white you now, I thought she was a nurse, and I asked if I could see Cole. But she returned and said "Tomorrow. He has his leg off." Well, that was it. I was leaving that night so I didn't see him.

I had had a good visit with him a couple of years before in New York. He went to the hospital, that place up the Hudson there, quite a ways. He was there for a long time and apparently, from what I heard, he didn't really have to be there, he just began to like it. And you know there is something about a hospital, you feel very protected and you're taken care of and he had a nice room. His secretary told me he'd like to see me. We talked mostly about family. It was good.

During the course of my interview with Ted Fetter, he told me something quite extraordinary. He said Cole once told him that Linda had been pregnant with his child, but that she had had a miscarriage.

NEDDA LOGAN: Just before the very sad end, Cole called asking Josh and me to come for dinner that very night. We were both very reluctant but he seemed so depressed we hated to let him down. All through dinner he ate very little and barely said a word. Following dinner, the waiter set up a card table in his room and we all seated ourselves around it, enabling him to be closer to us.

Both Josh and I talked about things we felt would interest and amuse him; small talk about mutual friends in and out of the theater. The more casual and intimate setting made little difference; Cole was just not up to handling conversation. There was little of his legendary sparkle that night. It was so sad. Josh and I did not see him again.

BROOKE ASTOR: I don't want to talk about those last sad years of his life because it was not his fault. . . .

ON MAY 15, 1960, a tribute sponsored by the Children's Asthma Research Institute and Hospital in Denver created a Cole Porter Research Fund at a "Salute to Cole Porter" at the Metropolitan Opera House. The tribute to the veteran composer was conceived and coordinated by Earl Blackwell and featured appearances by Ethel Merman, Anita Loos, Helen Hayes, Vinton Freedly, Bella Spewack, Jimmy Durante, Bert Lahr, Noel Coward, Beatrice Lillie, Lisa Kirk, Clifton Webb, Moss Hart, and many others. Needless to say, Cole did not even entertain the idea of appearing. At this point in his life with the loss of his leg, he did not see anyone except for his close friends. Cole was an elegant, polished man, with more than a certain amount of vanity. He still had pride in the way he looked and when he wasn't looking well, he tended to shut himself away. He had always liked to show his best side.

Despite this gradual withdrawal, Cole maintained his usual yearly routine of living in New York from October to June. Every Friday noon he took off with his chauffeur and his valet and an occasional guest (few people could just pick up and leave on Friday noon and not return to New York until midday

Monday) and drove to Williamstown. Once at Buxton Hill, he stayed in the enlarged, renovated cottage that had been his studio, surrounded by his records of his original music scores and a tranquilizing view of the Berkshire Mountains.

On May 7, 1963, Cole Porter lost another friend—Monty Woolley, "The Man Who Came to Dinner." He died in Saratoga Springs at the age of 74.

Monty and Cole had a topsy-turvy relationship spanning fifty-six years. The bearded actor-director and friend of Cole's from their Yale days had shared almost every exploit of Cole's, and perhaps knew more about the composer's life than most of his friends. Now, Woolley's death went almost totally unnoticed, and according to friends, unlamented, by Cole Porter. Rumor had it that Cole became irritated with his onetime bosom pal when he learned that Woolley had taken his black manservant as a lover. Members of Cole's family dispute this reasoning. No one incident had put a strain on their friendship in the ten years prior to Monty's death. They just drifted apart; not an unusual circumstance in a relationship covering so many decades and surrounded by so many vicissitudes. I am inclined to believe that is what happened to their once inseparable relationship. This was confirmed when Cole's cousin, Ted Fetter, told me that he felt Monty and Cole had just drifted apart in the years prior to Woolley's death.

From June to October Cole kept up his transcontinental commute and spent the summer in his rented home in Brentwood. It was during one of these visits, in September 1964, that he entered St. John's Hospital in Santa Monica to prepare for an operation to remove a kidney stone.

The operation was successful but Cole had lost his will to live—the fun had gone out of life long ago, and now he looked forward to the end. It came at 11:05 P.M. on October 15, 1964.

The New York Times: Cole Porter is dead; songwriter was 72.

ELISE SMITH: The first Mother and I learned of Cole Porter's death was a 7:00 A.M. phone call we received from Cole's masseur, and the reason for the call was to determine if Mother knew just what had been left to people in Cole's will. This only six hours after the composer's death in California. We found his call quite shocking and it only reinforced Mother's low opinion of this character.

> I direct my executors to arrange for no funeral or memorial service but only for a private burial service to be conducted by the pastor of the First Baptist Church in Peru, in the presence of my relatives and dearest friends. At such a service I request said pastor to read the following quotation from the Bible:
>> "I am the resurrection and the life; he that believeth in me, though he were dead, yet shall he live; and whosoever liveth and believeth in me shall never die,"
> and follow such quotation with the Lord's Prayer.
>
> I request that the foregoing be substantially the entire burial service, and that neither said pastor nor anyone else deliver any memorial address whatsoever. I particularly direct that there be no service of any kind in New York City. . . .
>
> —Cole Porter

LEON ALLEN: Richard L. Murray, an employee and later partner in the Eikenberry-Murray Funeral Service [in Peru, Indiana], answered the telephone when a Pierce Brothers Mortuary in Santa Monica, California, called and said, "We are shipping you the body of Cole Porter." Mr. Murray remembers that the body was a small-framed thin man. His fingers were long and thin.

Graveside services only were conducted at Mt. Hope Cemetery at 2:30 P.M. Sunday, October 16, 1964. There was no service at the First Baptist Church nor was there a procession from the funeral home to the cemetery, but there were limousines and big cars all over the place. . . . A huge blanket of roses completely covered the casket and touched the ground.

<u>JAMES OMAR COLE:</u>   I remember vividly his burial service conducted by the pastor of the First Baptist Church of Peru.

I'll take you to the grave site at Mt. Hope Cemetery, where Cole lies buried between the two most important people in his life—Kate and Linda. The markers are made from native Vermont stone with just the names and the years of his birth and death carved into the stone.

The eyewitness comments of the funeral director, Leon Allen, and Cole's cousin, James Omar Cole, nullify the widely reported story that Cole Porter's body was cremated.

Thus, on a cold, rainy day in Peru, Cole Porter was returned to the uninviting northern Indiana landscape that had provided him with little more than his heritage; the rest he created out of his own genius.

The New York Sunday News: COLE PORTER'S MANY MILLIONS LEFT TO COUSIN AND FRIENDS. The multi-million dollar estate of songwriter Cole Porter will go to a first cousin, Jules Omar Cole of Peru, Indiana, and Jules' son, James, the composer's will, on file for probate in Surrogate's Court, disclosed yesterday.

Another cousin, Mrs. Kate Cole McCaffrey of Asheville, North Carolina, gets nothing. The two cousins were Cole's closest living relatives.

<u>JAMES OMAR COLE:</u>   His will was a remarkable document of twenty-nine pages. His will further showed that the year Cole spent at Harvard Law School had not been a total loss. He left all the original musical manuscripts to Yale. I feel Yale has not properly presented this material, not the way it should be. I guess institutions, when left things of this sort, have to have funds to maintain it.

Among the friends who received bequests: Fred Astaire's daughter Ave received the aquamarine and ruby necklace that formerly belonged to Linda; Mrs. William Goetz, the Cambodian head sculpture and a small watercolor painting of a seashore scene; Mrs. John C. Wilson (formerly Princess Natalie Paley of Russia), the Tchelitchew portrait of herself and $10,000; his faithful secretary, Mrs. Madeline P. Smith, received $10,000; his favorite cousin, Mrs. Hiram I. Bearss received a token $10,000; the Museum of Modern Art, New York, all the cigarette cases and the scrapbooks labeled "People"; Benjamin Sturges, a portrait of Howard Sturges; James Omar Cole, real estate and interest in the Music and Literary Property Trust; Jules Omar Cole, all articles of property, including cars and otherwise unbequeathed household furnishings; the Juilliard School of Music was left his Waldorf apartment pianos, and the Salvation Army received all his clothing; Douglas Fairbanks, Jr., was bequeathed a pearl and diamond evening shirt button (not, as reported in the newspapers, a diamond dress stud).

About this last bequest, James Omar Cole indicated that the famed actor and international socialite "bugged" the executors for months until he was finally given his bequest. But this last bequest has an interesting story and was not as James Omar Cole had indicated.

DOUGLAS FAIRBANKS, JR.: Of course my father knew him as well, but I am not sure how well, although they would frequently meet at parties or functions of mutual friends. I make this point because you noted that he bequeathed me his "favorite diamond evening stud." This generous act on his part was not exactly as you have recalled it. Actually, it was a pearl and diamond evening shirt button that belonged to my father. I had not even been conscious of its existence! But when my father died, my stepmother managed to acquire it somehow, and because she was so fond of Cole, *she* gave it to him. Before

[Cole] died he informed me that he was proud to have that shirt button, but was a bit mystified because he did not know my father all that well, and that he thought by rights I should have had it anyway, and not Sylvia. It was not for me to comment on this for obvious reasons. He then added that he was going to leave me the button in his will, so that if I outlived him it would be mine anyway. Indeed, I am not sure whether he actually wore the thing or not. As I have no evening shirt with only one buttonhole, I have never worn the darn thing either! Anyway, I was very touched by Cole's typically kind and generous thought, although it was a strange episode.

Another unusual legacy was the bequest giving Ray C. Kelly (a male nurse during the early days of Cole's post-accident period) a half-interest in Cole Porter's copyrighted music. Kelly, after leaving Cole's employ, rarely visited the composer in the last sad years of his life. The other half-interest in the copyrighted music went to the late Jules Omar Cole and his son, James.

Coda

THE LEGACY OF Cole Porter lies primarily where it should—in his music. Cole's treasury will live as long as anyone wants to listen to songs bearing a witty, sophisticated touch. Or songs that have a raucous joy. Or a haunting and voluptuous surrender.

Cole Porter without question is an acquired taste, but then so are caviar and champagne.

IRVING BERLIN: He was the greatest of us all.

FLORENCE LEEDS: He took the attitude well, "If you don't like this one, how about this one." If there's a criticism I could make of him, it was that he really didn't fight hard enough for some of his songs.

RICHARD SEVERO: Cole Porter wasn't perfect, only incomparable!

TRUMAN CAPOTE: And Cole adored champagne. God, I do miss Cole so, dotty as he was those last years. Did I ever tell you the story about Cole and the stud wine steward? I can't remember quite where he worked. He was Italian, so it couldn't have been here [La Côte Basque] or Pav [Le Pavillon]. The Colony? Odd: I see him clearly—a nut-brown man, beautifully flat, with oiled hair and the sexiest jawline—but I can't see where I see him. He was southern, so they called him Dixie. . . .

Cole's approach was creative: he invited Dixie to his apartment under the pretext of getting advice on the laying in of a new wine cellar—Cole! Who knew more about wine than that dago ever dreamed. So they were sitting there on the couch—the lovely suede one Billy Baldwin made for Cole—all very informal and Cole kisses this fellow on the cheek, and Dixie grins and says, "That will cost you five-hundred dollars, Mr. Porter." Cole just laughs and squeezes Dixie's leg. "Now that will cost you a thousand dollars, Mr. Porter." Then Cole realizes this piece of pizza was serious; and so he unzippered him, hauled him out, shook it and said, "What will be the full price on the use of that?" Dixie told him two-thousand dollars. Cole went straight to his desk, wrote a check and handed it to him. And he said, "Miss Otis regrets she's unable to lunch today. Now get out."

SHERIDAN MORLEY: Being a Porter addict rather than a Porter expert, I fear I do not have a lot to offer, except perhaps the thought that one of his oldest friends and admirers, Noel Coward, managed to say in fifty words rather more about Old King Cole than most critics have ever managed since. This was, in a cabaret at Las Vegas in 1955, the way Coward introduced, to what he called Nescafé Society, his classic rewrite of Porter's "Let's Do It":

> Mr. Irving Berlin
> Often emphasized sin
> In a charming way.

Mr. Coward we know
Wrote a song or two to show
Sex was here to stay.
Richard Rodgers it's true
Took a more romantic view
Of that sly biological urge,
But it really was Cole
Who contrived to make the whole
Thing merge.

STEPHEN SONDHEIM: I met Cole Porter in Williamstown once, when I was eighteen. I was brought to his house by Dr. Albert Sirmay (of Chappell) to play the score of a show we were doing up there, an adaptation I'd written of *Beggar on Horseback*. I have two major memories of that afternoon at Porter's house, the first being that it was the dead of winter and there was a sign outside the front door saying, "Please Wipe Feet; White Rugs Inside." The second memory is of Mr. Porter's extraordinary graciousness—he even advised me on how to extend the ending of a song called "The Bordelaise," which was a parody of every Porter beguine. In any event I came away from the afternoon exhilarated.

The only other time I met Mr. Porter was at his suite in the Waldorf-Astoria, where Jule Styne took me while we were writing *Gypsy*. It was at Anita Loos's request. She had called Jule to tell him that Porter was feeling depressed and that hearing a new score for Ethel [Merman] might cheer him up. As indeed it seemed to do. Jule and I played the seven songs we had written, and I took especial pleasure in hearing Porter's murmured cry of delight when he heard the punch on the quadruple rhyme ("amigos") in the release of "Together Wherever We Go." But this time I did not come away exhilarated because I could see that Porter was a dying man.

Certainly his reputation has maintained itself, but as a songwriter, not on the theatrical scene. Certainly, he's the equal of his contemporaries. As for his shows being revived, it's not their topicality that's bothersome, but their "old-fashionedness," which is true of most shows written prior to Rodgers and Hammerstein.

I love a lot of Porter's work but no, he hasn't influenced me (that I'm aware of). I've used his style for pastiches occasionally, but I think that's it.

TED FETTER: It's just too bad that there isn't a more understanding and respectful attitude towards the legacy of Cole. Cole is and was one of the greats of the so-called golden era of musical comedy, there's no question about it. He could've been a hell of a musician, too, and he wrote good music. He had a style unmistakably Porter. Now once in a while you'll hear something and say, "That sounds like Porter." It may not be Porter but it sounds like Porter because he had this wonderful style of—he characterized it to Dick Rodgers as "writing Jewish"—it has an insinuating kind of semantic feel to it. He could write really upbeat-type-of music, too.

MICHAEL CORDA: I don't think it's money alone that has prevented a revival of Cole's shows on broadway. People are still around who loved him and grew up appreciating his music. It has more to do with the total lack of quality in the music being dispensed today. The music business has regressed to a new low. *Kiss Me, Kate* was the first musical to win a "Tony" and now you have the likes of [country music] winning a "Tony." It makes you realize that Broadway has hit a new low.

RICHARD ADLER: He was a remarkable man! And do you know the way I met him? I was at my barber and was summoned to take a telephone call. The caller said, "This is Cole Porter," and thinking this was my friend Sammy Davis, I responded, "This is Irving Berlin." He said, "No, no, no, this *is* Cole Porter" in that crisp, high-pitched voice, just at the moment when I was about to call him a dirty name. He was merely calling to invite me to Michael's Pub that evening. He was going to see *Damn Yankees* for the fifth time, and I got skeptical; that show was fine but I never in my life went to a show five times.

We developed a close friendship and I visited him many times at his Waldorf Towers apartment. There on his piano was a container filled with pencils, all exactly the same height and all sharpened to a pinpoint, and I thought, holy smokes, somebody really is doing a job here. And I guess it was part of his compulsive nature to have the pencils all sharpened to exactly the same size.

In his probing of me as to how I write, he told me he writes a song every day of his life no matter what. He has to write a song every day of his life! That doesn't mean they were good songs, but there must be hundreds of them. I am the opposite. I work only when there is a project, and then I work full time on it.

Cole had the ability of being able to write the most sophisticated hooks and yet the simplest. Not only that, he also wrote what we call "music footballs," you know, colons. The singer can really get into it and belt it out.

We had a very good time, Cole and I together, we exchanged thoughts all the time and joked a lot. Cole was so articulate and so knowledgeable about art and out of the ordinary, extremely elegant parts of the world, domiciles, whatever, that very few people would even think about, and he could talk about anything.

On one visit with Cole, he asked me questions for about an hour or so and I thought, "Well hell, I better ask him some questions, too." So I said what about this wonderful song, "All of You." I was just fascinated with it. And this line, "the east, west, north, and the south of you." Isn't that a Porter "sexy line"—"the south of you"—what else could it be? And "I'd love to gain complete control of you, and handle even the heart and soul of you." That's an agent's word. And I said to him, "You really wrote a character song, because you were writing a song to get into the kind of character Don Ameche was."

ARDIS KRAINIK: It is hard to elaborate musically about my passion for *The Gay Divorcée* because the major reason I love it is because of Ginger Rogers's and Fred Astaire's superb dancing. I own all their movies, but obviously there cannot be great dancing without great music and Cole Porter was the greatest.

As a young singer, the songs of Cole Porter were to me the most beautiful songs ever written. They were popular songs, yes, but they had a depth about them, a sophistication, a real musical profundity that has proved itself over the years, for today they are still living and breathing and palpitating, just as they did in the year that Cole Porter wrote them.

In the late '40s and 1950s, as a young singer, I sang Cole Porter songs on every single program I did, beginning as a teenager, and as a matter of fact, right up to the last day I sang a professional note in 1977. My favorites were: "Night and Day," "Begin the Beguine," "Another Op'nin', Another Show," "So In Love," "What Is This Thing Called Love," "You're the Top," and "My Heart Belongs to Daddy."

A Cole Porter song always concluded every recital and program that I did, and as a matter of fact, were much more popular with the audiences than the opera arias I sang! My favorite was "Night and Day." It won me every audition, and lots of jobs that kept [me] alive from 1954 to 1960.

Now I am the general manager of a great opera company [the Lyric Opera of Chicago], but I still sing Cole Porter every summer. Our entire company is invited to the home of our secretary and general counsel of the Board of Directors, Lee Freeman . . . [and] I am always asked to bring my music, because I have all the Cole Porter songs! All of the young people in our school, the Lyric Opera Center for American Artists, sing Cole Porter songs today. Every once in a while, the general manager is forced to sing along with the group. So, Cole Porter lives in my heart and in my life in a way that is, perhaps, a little unexpected.

The special sophistication of Cole Porter was evident not only in his music, but particularly in his lyrics—such sophisticated lyrics, lending themselves to such marvelous expression by singers who really know how to express words. This is, after all, what music drama or musical theater are all about—a grand story, a beautiful libretto, a wonderful text set to glorious music, and Cole Porter did all of this. His works were great vehicles for the greatest performers of his time—and ours.

JAMES OMAR COLE: His music remains so fresh today. Unlike Victor Herbert, whose music died with the man. I would say that only Gershwin occupies an equal place in American music.

FRANK SINATRA: During a particularly slow Sunday night at the Rustic Cabin, my drummer leaned over and said, "Cole Porter is in the audience."

I had been so infatuated with his music, I couldn't believe he was sitting out there. I dedicated the next song, "Night and Day," to Mr. Porter. The orchestra played the introduction and I proceeded to forget all the words. I kept singing "Night and Day" for fifteen bars.

Many years later, I got to know Mr. Porter quite well, and we were doing a film [*High Society*] with the late Grace Kelly and Bing Crosby. And he called me aside and said, "I don't know if you remember meeting me at some nightclub you were working."

I said, "Oh yeah." And he said, "So do I. That's about the worst performance I ever heard."

In music circles it was generally known that Cole Porter was never quite happy with Frank Sinatra's interpretation of his music; among other things, he resented the dooby-dooby-doos the singer would intersperse among his lyrics. But then Cole felt much the same way about many singers who re-interpreted his words. In his estimation, there was no one quite like Ethel Merman when it came to rendering a Cole Porter lyric.

He did, however, admire the artistry of Lena Horne, Mabel Mercer, and, to a degree, Bricktop, but Cole rarely gave a salute to a male vocalist.

That long-ago performance at the Rustic Cabin notwithstanding, if Cole Porter were alive today he would acknowledge a debt of gratitude to Frank Sinatra. Of all the pop singers of the mid-twentieth century, Sinatra has given the greatest interpretation to Porter's music. It is this mature Frank Sinatra who brought the necessary elegance that matched Cole Porter's classy lyrics.

Frank Sinatra's own admiration for the composer has gone beyond the musical scene; his Manhattan residence is the former Cole Porter apartment at the Waldorf Towers.

STEPHEN HANDZO: As Kern is the greatest romantic and Berlin is the greatest primitive, Porter remains the supreme sophisticate of American song.

PAUL LAZARUS: For our version [the Goodspeed Opera House] of *You Never Know,* we have gone back to the original manuscript of the book: reconstructing the show in the scale and spirit intended by the authors. In essence, this "romantic farce with songs" is a rehabilitated version: it is not a revival of what was seen at the Winter Garden Theater in 1938, but what we feel Porter and Leigh really wanted.

We have reinstated several songs Cole Porter wrote, but which were dropped during the show's pre-Broadway tryout:

"By Candlelight," "I'm Going In For Love" and "I'm Back In Circulation" fall into that category.

<u>MOSS HART:</u> He burst upon that moribund world with the velocity of a meteor streaking across the sky.

<u>RICHARD ADLER:</u> The man was a school in himself. A school with no students. Other songwriters can be imitated, but not Cole Porter.

The New York Times: The hallmark of a typical Porter song was lyrics that were urbane or witty and a melody with a sinuous brooding quality. Some of his best-known songs in this vein were "This Thing Called Love," "Love For Sale" and "Begin the Beguine." But equally typical and equally recognizable Porter songs would have a single, bouncy melody and a lyric based on a long entertaining list of similarities, opposites or contrasts. "Let's Do It, Let's Fall In Love," ticked off the amiable amatory habits of birds, flowers, fish, insects, animals and various types of humans, while "You're the Top" was an exercise in the creation of superlatives that included such items as "the nimble thread of the feet of Fred Astaire," and "Garbo's salary" and "Mickey Mouse."

THE MEMORY OF Cole Porter in the more than twenty years since his death is one that is woven into the legend of the American musical theater and the one that remains with us today.

That his music remains almost as popular today as when he wrote it is due in large measure to the quality of his work—a monumental contribution to the world of music.

When a definitive history of music is written, there will be more than a chapter devoted to the five composers who constitute the zenith among American popular songwriters. The five: George Gershwin, Irving Berlin, Jerome Kern, Richard Rodgers, and Cole Porter. Their music has become world famous and is constantly revived fifty or more years after much of it was conceived. Among these five, Cole Porter was the only one who wrote both the words *and* the music.

Cole Porter put fizz to his music and lyrics, enabling people to take flight on gossamer wings. He reminded the public that one sniff of cocaine would bore him terrific-ly, too. For the deserted and depressed, he encouraged them to dream about the crowds punishing the parquet at El Morocco. It was his cajoling of the public over a fifty-year span to "Let's Do It, Let's Fall in Love" that has allowed his reputation to endure. His magic continues to color our lives today, giving each of us who listen to a Cole Porter melody an opportunity to recapture a special moment in life and an added reason for living and loving.

MADELINE P. SMITH: On October 15, 1964, Cole Porter died . . . at the age of 73. But his memory lingers on and on and on. Such genius cannot be forgotten. Even now . . . there is a constant resurgence of tributes to his memory, constant repetitions of his songs. . . . A talent of such magnitude will live forever. And I was there. What a privilege!

Biographical Notes

GEORGE ABBOTT, playwright, director, and producer, staged Cole Porter's 1938 show *You Never Know*. The ninety-nine year-old Broadway legend recently finished directing one of his early successes, *On Your Toes*, in San Francisco.

RICHARD ADLER met Cole Porter in the 1950s, and the two composers became close friends. Mr. Adler is a two-time Tony Award winner and perhaps best known for *The Pajama Game* and *Damn Yankees*. Of late he has turned his attention to symphonic works.

THE DUCHESS OF ALBA, Maria del Rosario Cayetana Fitz-James Stuart, is the daughter of Cole and Linda's late, great friend "Jimmy" de Alba. She is not only the Duchess of Alba but also the Duchess of Berwick in the Scottish peerage. Cayetana de Alba holds forty-seven titles and is eighteen times a grandee of Spain.

LADY SYLVIA ASHLEY is the widow of Douglas Fairbanks, Sr., and a friend of Cole and Linda Porter.

BROOKE ASTOR, author, doyenne of New York's social and philanthropic circles and president of the Vincent Astor Foundation, first met Cole Porter in 1928 while married to Charles (Buddie) Marshall. She remained a close friend until the composer's death.

BILLY BALDWIN was a friend of the Porters for many years and a spectacularly successful interior designer.

MAXINE FOGELMAN BATEMAN served as Cole Porter's secretary in Williamstown, Massachusetts during a period of time. She is a Peru, Indiana, native.

LUCIUS BEEBE was a proper Bostonian and well-known man about the world who for many years was a columnist for *The New York Herald-Tribune*.

IRVING BERLIN, the dean of American composers, was, with his wife Ellin, a friend of the Porters from the 1920s on. He never missed a chance to see a Cole Porter show and never failed to wire congratulations to Cole when a show opened.

EARL BLACKWELL is the founder of Celebrity Service and was a contributing editor to *Town & Country*. Mr. Blackwell is as much of a celebrity as the ones he tracks through his international registry. He is also a novelist.

FANNY BRICE was a star of the Ziegfeld Follies, a singer, and a comedienne during the 1920s and '30s. She later gained more fame on radio as "Baby Snooks." Her life was depicted in the Broadway show and film *Funny Girl*. Fanny Brice often visited the Porters in Paris and Venice.

BRICKTOP, née Ada Beatrice Queen Victoria Louise Virginia Smith, was a famous nightclub owner and entertainer to a generation of expatriate Americans in post-World War I Paris and, later, in Rome. The Chicago-reared singer was befriended by Cole Porter soon after she opened her first club.

ABE BURROWS was the playwright and director of *Can-Can* as well as many other well-known Broadway productions.

JAMES OMAR COLE, second cousin of Cole Porter and his closest living relative, is a lawyer and now resides near Peru, Indiana, in Westleigh Farms, Cole Porter's mother's home.

PETER COOKSON, a distinguished American actor, co-starred in *Can-Can*. He is married to actress Beatrice Straight.

MIKE CORDA was part of the original pit orchestra for *Kiss Me, Kate*. He is a bassist and composer.

NOEL COWARD, actor, playwright, screenwriter, composer, and author, was sometimes dubbed "the British Cole Porter." Coward was the only individual in the world of show business and society during the thirties whose stature as a celebrity equaled that of Cole Porter. The two men remained lifelong friends after first meeting in Europe during the 1920s. In addition to Coward's original compositions, he also did a number of parodies of Cole Porter songs.

HOWARD CULLMAN was a Yale classmate and lifelong friend of Cole Porter. A socially prominent Manhattan businessman, he was also one of the biggest financial backers of *Kiss Me, Kate*.

PEMBROKE DAVENPORT, musical director of a number of Cole Porter's shows including *Kiss Me, Kate*, later mounted shows in Las Vegas where he died under mysterious circumstances.

ALFRED DE LIAGRE, JR., was another Yaleman and a friend of both Cole Porter and Monty Woolley. He later went on to become one of the most famous Broadway producers.

ROSIE DOLLY, one-half of the legendary Dolly Sisters, knew Cole Porter from the 1920s on. Cole composed "Two Little Babes in the Wood" for her and her sister, Jenny, to sing in *Greenwich Village Follies* (1924). The Dolly Sisters socialized with the composer in Paris and Venice, and at one point Jenny's then-paramour, merchant prince Gordon Selfridge, offered to back a show for the Dolly Sisters if Cole would compose the entire score.

DOUGLAS FAIRBANKS, JR., actor, producer, writer, and corporate director, first met Cole Porter during the 1920s. The handsome, debonair Knight Commander of the British Empire traveled in the same social circles as Porter in the States and abroad. He and his wife, Mary Lee Fairbanks, were Cole's friends until the time of his death.

TED FETTER, Cole's cousin (Cole's grandfather and Ted's grandmother were brother and sister) and the only other member of the family to be in the entertainment business. He has had a long career as an entertainment consultant, actor, lyricist (including "Taking a Chance on Love"), and television executive.

MARGARET CASE HARRIMAN was a longtime staff member of *The New Yorker*. It was Miss Harriman who made the magazine's "Profiles" an art form.

W. AVERELL HARRIMAN, a former governor of New York and ambassador to both the USSR and Great Britain, first met Cole at Yale. Gov. Harriman was a longtime supporter of Democratic Party causes, and his widow, Pamela C. Harriman, continues his endeavors.

HELEN HAYES, the distinguished American actress, knew Cole Porter from his first, early successful Broadway shows and with her late husband, Charles MacArthur, saw Porter in New York and Hollywood.

TOMMY HENDRICKS was one of Cole Porter's few boyhood friends from Peru, Indiana. Despite the fact that Mr. Hendricks later went to Princeton, he and the composer remained friends until Cole moved to Europe. Tommy Hendricks became a well-known Indiana businessman.

ROBERT KIMBALL is a Yale graduate, author, and consultant to the Cole Porter Musical and Literary Property Trusts. He has edited a number of books on the musical works of the composer.

ARDIS KRAINIK is general manager of Chicago's Lyric Opera. Before heading this well-known opera company, she sang with the company and had a distinguished career as a concert singer.

JOHN LAHR is a well-known author and drama critic and the son of the late Bert Lahr.

FLORENCE LEEDS, the executive secretary of the Cole Porter Musical and Literary Trusts, is the point person when it comes to obtaining information about the composer's works in the theater and in motion pictures.

RICHARD LEWINE was the producer of Cole Porter's only television offering, "Aladdin".

<u>NEDDA HARRIGAN LOGAN</u> and her husband, director Joshua Logan, were longtime friends of the composer. Mrs. Logan was an actress before marriage and a prominent Manhattan hostess.

<u>CHARLES ("BUDDIE") MARSHALL</u> was a classmate and friend of Cole's and a prominent New York stockbroker. He was an unusually kind man and was the brother-in-law of two of the most powerful men in America, publisher Marshall Field III and Vincent Astor.

<u>MARY MARTIN</u> first gained fame on Broadway singing a Cole Porter song and, from that moment on, continued to make Broadway history.

<u>ELSA MAXWELL</u> began her career playing piano in theaters that featured silent movies. Despite her lack of good looks, money, education, and social position, she became a renowned international celebrity publicist and party hostess. Though she lived completely by her wits and had an ego to match her large body, she also had the blessed ability to laugh at herself. Elsa often annoyed Cole Porter with her less-than-honorable methods for turning a fast buck, but they always kissed and made up, and they had a long friendship.

<u>ETHEL MERMAN</u> appeared in five of Cole Porter's Broadway hits and became his all-time favorite singer.

<u>HAZEL MEYER</u> is a well-known authority in the music field and author of a number of books on popular music.

<u>ROBERT MONTGOMERY</u> is a lawyer and a trustee of the Cole Porter Musical and Literary Property Trusts. He also represents composer Stephen Sondheim.

<u>PATRICIA MORISON</u>   won stardom in *Kiss Me, Kate.* She occasionally returns to the stage but devotes most of her time in Los Angeles to her career as a painter.

<u>ROBERT MORLEY</u>   is music critic for the British publication *Punch* and author of a number of books, including one on Noel Coward.

<u>PATRICE MUNSEL,</u>   diva of the Metropolitan Opera Company, met Cole Porter late in his career and often appeared in a number of his shows on the road and in summer stock.

<u>GERALD MURPHY</u>   was a Yale classmate and may have been Cole Porter's first real friend at that school. Heir to the Mark Cross leather fortune, he had little inclination for business and after leaving Yale joined other expatriate Americans in Paris during post-World War I. Later, he established a beachhead on the French Riviera where his Villa America became a mecca for both American and European artists, writers, and ballet company members. Gerald Murphy and his wife, Sara, were the inspiration for the F. Scott Fitzgerald characters Dick and Nicole Diver in *Tender Is the Night.* Sara adored Cole but felt less kindly toward Linda.

<u>NATASHA PALEY</u>   was a princess of the Russian Imperial family and related to half the crowned heads of Europe. Her first husband was couturier Lucian Lelong. Later, she married Jack Wilson. Natasha was an intimate friend of both Cole and Linda Porter.

<u>LOUELLA PARSONS</u>   was the number-one Hollywood gossip columnist of her day and a longtime friend and admirer of Cole Porter. She made and broke careers with a stroke of her pen.

SCHUYLER LIVINGSTON PARSONS   was one of the bluest of the blueblooded Hudson River Valley aristocracy. He was first a friend of Linda Porter and later of Cole. Parsons knew everybody and went everywhere on both sides of the Atlantic. When he lost his fortune he ended his days as a stock clerk in a Palm Beach grocery-liquor store but still was received and accepted by the grande dames of that uppercrust resort town.

MICHAEL PEARMAN   was the founder of the popular Michael's Pub in Manhattan. Cole Porter was an early financial backer of his friend's establishment. The former actor is presently an antique dealer in Palm Beach.

KATE PORTER   was Cole Porter's mother. Her early efforts with her only surviving child steered him toward a musical career.

LINDA LEE PORTER,   wife of Cole Porter, made beauty do for her what the lack of money could not—take her to the upper rungs of the social world. Men of such divergent views as the Duke of Alba and Winston Churchill found her fascinating. To the casual observer, Linda and Cole were an odd couple, leading separate lives most of their married life. A marriage like theirs can best be understood (and lived) only by the very rich.

TOM PRIDEAUX   was a longtime observer of Cole Porter and his theater and film efforts. He was the former entertainment editor for *Life* magazine and the author of a biography of James McNeill Whistler.

ARTIE SHAW'S   rendition of "Begin the Beguine" made it a top moneymaker for him and the composer. His recording continues to have healthy sales today. Mr. Shaw is a clarinetist, bandleader, writer, and man of many other talents.

LOUIS SHURR   was a New York theatrical agent and the first one to take a chance on the untried talents of a then-unknown Cole Porter.

ELSIE SMITH   is the daughter of Cole Porter's longtime secretary Madeline P. Smith. She is on the staff of the Center for Human Rights at the United Nations.

MADELINE P. SMITH   served as Cole Porter's personal secretary for seventeen years. Before her association with Porter, she was social secretary to Lady Sylvia Ashley (widow of Douglas Fairbanks, Sr.), and secretary to the Belgian ambassador to the United States. She was awarded the Order of the Crown by the king of Belgium for her work.

LOUIS SOBEL   was the dean of Broadway columnists and a longtime observer and admirer of the composer's talents.

STEPHEN SONDHEIM,   composer and lyricist (*Gypsy, West Side Story, A Little Night Music, Sunday in the Park with George* are some of his credits), first met Cole Porter while a student at Williams College.

BELLA SPEWACK   and her husband, Sam, were the creators of *Boy Meets Girl* and *Kiss Me, Kate*. Bella is a warm, exuberant woman who almost singlehandedly prodded Cole Porter back to work after a series of Broadway flops.

BENJAMIN R. STURGES   is a nephew of the late Howard Sturges, a member of one of Rhode Island's most distinguished families, and a well-known financial consultant in his native city of Providence, R.I.

HOWARD STURGES   was a bon vivant international traveler and great friend of Linda Porter and subsequently a friend of Cole.

GENEVIEVE TOBIN   was the co-star of Cole Porter's *Fifty Million Frenchmen.* Today the former musical star lives in Manhattan within view of the Metropolitan Museum but a long way from Broadway.

GWEN VERDON   is the third performer to become an overnight Broadway sensation after appearing in a Cole Porter show. Among her other credits are *Damn Yankees* and *Sweet Charity.* In recent years she has divided her energies between movies and assisting former husband Bob Fosse in choreographing his musicals.

DIANA VREELAND   knew both Linda and Cole Porter socially during the 1920s. Known as the Empress of Fashion because of her years with *Harper's Bazaar* and as editor-in-chief of *Vogue,* she now acts as consultant to the Costume Institute of the Metropolitan Museum of Art.

ARNOLD WHITRIDGE   was a Yale classmate and lifelong friend of the composer. The distinguished author and historian was very active in the Yale Dramat during his student days; one of the songs he and Cole introduced at Yale was Porter's "Rolling, Rolling."

WALTER WINCHELL   originated the gossip column. For many years his column in the *New York Daily Mirror* was the most widely read feature in America's newspapers. A word from Winchell could make or break a Broadway show. He was a great fan of Cole Porter and through his column widely promoted the composer and his shows.

<u>MONTY (EDGAR MONTILLION) WOOLLEY</u> befriended the future Broadway composer when Cole Porter first set foot on the Yale campus. Porter credits Woolley with directing him toward a career in the theater. The actor/director, known almost as much for his beard as for his wit, once said beards were "the historic trademark of genius." His greatest moment in the theater was his role as the arrogant and waspish Sheridan Whiteside in *The Man Who Came to Dinner,* a role he also played in the film version. In *Night and Day,* the screen biography of his friend, Monty played himself, possibly the only believable character in the film.

Acknowledgments

THE FIRST ACKNOWLEDGMENT must obviously go to the late Cole Porter, without whom, for so many reasons, this book would never have been written.

Next I should like to thank my literary agent, Agnes Birnbaum, whose vision and unstinting support made the burden and joy of writing easier. A special thanks to my very supportive editor, Liz Kelly, and the entire management and staff of Stein and Day.

I am greatly indebted to Brooke Astor for providing me with an invaluable appraisal of Cole Porter based on thirty-five years of friendship. Mrs. Astor's charm and conversational skill served as an inspiration to me.

This book and the final form it took would not have occurred had I not had the able and diligent contribution of my editorial assistant, Marshall Rens.

A further debt of gratitude is owed to Stephen Birmingham, in whose Cincinnati home the idea for this book first took form.

I am also indebted to the many individuals contacted, interviewed, and depended upon for the research that is so important to this book: Monty Woolley, for imparting a remembrance of Cole spanning almost sixty years of their friendship; Gwen Verdon, who was so generous with her time and her remembrance of Cole Porter; Douglas Fairbanks, Jr., whose response to this project was immediate; Peter Cookson, for his poignant memoir of the composer; Richard Adler for an "insider's" view of the composer; Ted Fetter, for his remembrance of his cousin; the late W. Averell Harriman for his remembrance of Cole from their Yale days; Robert Montgomery, trustee of The Cole Porter Musical and Literary Property Trusts, for his generous assistance and his permission to use various materials relating to Cole Porter; James Omar Cole, Cole's closest living relative, for his generosity of spirit and his immediate response to my requests; Arnold Whitridge; Pamela C. Harriman; The Duchess of Alba, for her wonderful childhood memories of Cole Porter; Alfred de Liagre, Jr.; George Abbott; the late Rosie Dolly; Beatrice Straight; Benjamin R. Sturges; Mike Corda; Stephen Sondheim; Richard Lewine; Patrice Munsel; the late Benny Goodman; Genevieve Tobin Keighley; the late Tommy Hendricks; Sheridan Morley; Madeline P. Smith; Elise Smith; Patricia Morison; Ardis Krainik; Tom Prideaux; Lisa Kirk; Diana Vreeland; Nedda Logan, and the late Bricktop, who during a week's stay in Chicago provided this writer with extensive background material relating to her longtime friendship with Cole and Linda Porter.

I would also like to thank Florence Leeds, executive secretary of the Trusts, for all her willing assistance and for arranging permission to use material at Yale and the New York Public Library's Theatre Collection; Shaun Granum, assistant curator of the Miami County Historical Society (Peru, Indiana) for placing at my disposal their extensive collection of Cole Porter memorabilia; Bill Wepler, curator, and Betty Richards, first vice-president of the Miami County Historical Society; John Adnay, editor of the *Peru Daily Tribune* for his assistance in giving access to that newspaper's files on Cole Porter and the

Porter and Cole families; Earl Blackwell (Celebrity Service); Diana Edkins (Conde-Nast Publications); John Hammond; John B. Fairchild (Fairchild Publications); Dorothy Swerdlove, curator of the Billy Rose Theatre Collection, the New York Public Library; Patricia Sanford (Cartier); Richard Warren, curator, Historical Sound Recordings, Yale; Mary Corliss (The Museum of Modern Art), Lisa Onofri (Museum of theCity of New York); Musée des Arts Decoratifs (Paris); Michael J. Arlen; Linda Gillies; Bill Campbell; Jerome Zerbe; Helen Hayes; Paul Lazarus, and Mary Martin.

Thanks also to Jean Barkhorn (*Town and Country*); Ann Buchwald; Artie Shaw; Nat Andriani (Wide World Photos); Michael Pearman; Lena Horne; the late Billy Baldwin; Sotheby's; the late Lil Hardin Armstrong, and Estelle Shapiro.

Friendships developed over many years have been an important factor in the completion of this book: Mariano Vidal Armstrong, for introducing this writer to the "right people" in Puerto Rico; Maria Roman-Lopez, my charming and considerate hostess on my annual sojourn to the island; Raul Solivan Torres, for his sustained friendship; Guillermo Cardona Solivan for his generous friendship over the years; Margot Arbona; José Clemente Gonzalez; Jorge Vendrell, Jr.; Pedro Vincenty; Ada Rita Valdevivieso de Matos; Yasmin Valdevivieso; Lila Mayoral de Hernandez; Carmen Diaz; William and Nikki Von Hoene; Edward Lahniers; Frances Collin; Richard McDonough; David Rich; Byron D. Starr; M. F. Hoffman; June K. Robinson; Mark Singer; Prince Muhammado Maccido; Madelaine Dosal de Machuca; Maybeth Dosal de Martinez; Robert Breving; Vernon and Carmen Rhinehart; Joy Bell; Emmanuel Caldwell; the late Betsy Crilly; Alfred and Jeanette Stern; Luis Rafael Sanchez; Alfred del Valle; Olgui Vassallo; John and Yvette Spaght; Clarisa Moscoso Moscoso; Jose de Jesus; Bob Cordova; Jose Ramon Mendez; Aurora L. Roman; Lucilla Gomez; Dorothy Frazier; William R. Clarke; Bob Djahanguiri; Anne

McCamet; Navin Deo; Lisa Baldonado; Jane Menich; Gladys and Jeffrey Strong; Edgar Himel; Anne Thompson; Lowell and Larry Zollar; Richard Sullivan; Ann Gerber; the entire Roman-Lopez clan; Hon. Luis Ferre; Carmen and Tito Castro; the late Mr. and Mrs. Angel Sanz; Geri Norington; and especially to Daryl Williams for his support and counsel during the entire project.

I am also indebted to the following authors and publishers for material important to this book:

Chicago Tribune, October 15, 1937, and April 30, 1984. Copyright © by the Chicago Tribune Company. All rights reserved.

Newsweek. May 18, 1953.

The New York Daily News

The New Yorker

The New York Times. Copyright © 1929/37/40/41/43/64/71/84 by The New York Times Company.

Time magazine

Materials from the following songs used by permission:

"All of You." Copyright © 1954 by Cole Porter; Copyright renewed by Chappell & Co.

"Bingo Eli Yale." Copyright © 1910 by Cole Porter. Copyright not renewed.

"Let's Do It." Copyright © 1928 by Warner Bros. Inc. Copyright renewed. All rights reserved.

"Miss Otis Regrets (She's Unable to Lunch Today)," Copyright © 1934 by Warner Bros. Inc. Copyright renewed. All rights reserved.

Photographs credited to Yale University are from the American Musical Theatre Collection, the Yale Collection of Historical Sound Recordings, Sterling Memorial Library, New Haven, Connecticut.

Photographs credited to the Cole Porter Collection are from the Cole Porter Musical and Literary Property Trusts.

Note: Every effort has been made to trace copyright holders of material used in this book. The publishers apologize if any material has been included without permission.